EMILY DICKINSON
SELECTED POEMS AND LETTERS

EMILY DICKINSON
SELECTED POEMS AND LETTERS

a *Broadview Anthology of American Literature* edition

Contributing Editors, *Emily Dickinson: Selected Poems and Letters*:
Don LePan, Nora Ruddock, and Helena Snopek

General Editors, *The Broadview Anthology of American Literature*:
Derrick R. Spires, Cornell University
Rachel Greenwald Smith, Saint Louis University
Christina Roberts, Seattle University
Joseph Rezek, Boston University
Justine S. Murison, University of Illinois, Urbana-Champaign
Laura L. Mielke, University of Kansas
Christopher Looby, University of California, Los Angeles
Rodrigo Lazo, University of California, Irvine
Alisha Knight, Washington College
Hsuan L. Hsu, University of California, Davis
Michael Everton, Simon Fraser University
Christine Bold, University of Guelph

broadview press

BROADVIEW PRESS – www.broadviewpress.com
Peterborough, Ontario, Canada

Founded in 1985, Broadview Press remains a wholly independent publishing house. Broadview's focus is on academic publishing: our titles are accessible to university and college students as well as scholars and general readers. With over 800 titles in print, Broadview has become a leading international publisher in the humanities, with world-wide distribution. Broadview is committed to environmentally responsible publishing and fair business practices.

Library and Archives Canada Cataloguing in Publication

Title: Emily Dickinson : selected poems and letters / contributing editors, Emily Dickinson: selected poems and letters, Don LePan, Nora Ruddock, and Helena Snopek ; general editors, The Broadview anthology of American literature: Derrick R. Spires (Cornell University), Rachel Greenwald Smith (Saint Louis University), Christina Roberts (Seattle University), Joseph Rezek (Boston University), Justine S. Murison (University of Illinois, Urbana-Champaign), Laura L. Mielke (University of Kansas), Christopher Looby (University of California, Los Angeles), Rodrigo Lazo (University of California, Irvine), Alisha Knight (Washington College), Hsuan L. Hsu (University of California, Davis), Michael Everton (Simon Fraser University), Christine Bold (University of Guelph).
Other titles: Works. Selections (2023)
Names: Dickinson, Emily, 1830-1886, author. | LePan, Don, 1954- editor. | Ruddock, Nora, 1978- editor. | Snopek, Helena, editor. | Spires, Derrick Ramon, editor.
Description: Series statement: A Broadview anthology of American literature edition | Includes bibliographical references and index.
Identifiers: Canadiana (print) 20230154379 | Canadiana (ebook) 20230154387 | ISBN 9781554816347 (softcover) | ISBN 9781770488953 (PDF) | ISBN 9781460408278 (EPUB)
Subjects: LCSH: Dickinson, Emily, 1830-1886—Poetry. | LCSH: Dickinson, Emily, 1830-1886—Correspondence. | LCGFT: Poetry. | LCGFT: Personal correspondence.
Classification: LCC PS1541 .A6 2023 | DDC 811/.4—dc23

Broadview Press handles its own distribution in North America:
PO Box 1243, Peterborough, Ontario K9J 7H5, Canada
555 Riverwalk Parkway, Tonawanda, NY 14150, USA
Tel: (705) 743-8990; Fax: (705) 743-8353
email: customerservice@broadviewpress.com

For all territories outside of North America, distribution is handled by Eurospan Group.

Broadview Press acknowledges the financial
support of the Government of Canada
for our publishing activities.

Canada

Developmental Editors: Don LePan, Nora Ruddock, and Helena Snopek
Cover Designer: Lisa Brawn
Typesetter: Alexandria Stuart

PRINTED IN CANADA

Contents

EMILY DICKINSON

1830 – 1886

Emily Dickinson wrote in a letter to a friend that "Biography first convinces us of the fleeing of the Biographied—." And indeed, as several generations of critics and biographers have approached this enigmatic poet's work and life, the poet herself remains elusive, though legends about her abound. Widely considered one of America's greatest writers, Dickinson has attracted a dedicated and passionate readership, as well as worldwide critical acclaim. Working entirely in compact poetic forms, she left us close to 1,800 poems, among which are some of the most incisive and psychologically powerful lyrics in English on the subjects of death, love, nature, and religion.

Emily Elizabeth Dickinson was born in Amherst, in the Connecticut Valley of Massachusetts, on 10 December 1830, and for most of her life she continued to live with her family in an Amherst mansion called the Homestead. She was the second of three children to Edward and Emily Norcross Dickinson. Edward Dickinson was a locally prominent lawyer and politician, who entered the United States House of Representatives in 1853. He was also a pious man who regularly read to his children from the Bible; Dickinson later said of him that "his heart was pure and terrible, and I think no other like it exists." Dickinson's mother, Emily Norcross Dickinson, came from a family that valued education for women, and she herself studied the sciences intently while at school. She suffered ill health throughout her life, and seems to have been emotionally distant; Dickinson said to Thomas Wentworth Higginson in 1870 that she "never had a mother. I suppose a mother is one to whom you hurry when you are troubled."

In 1840, Dickinson and her sister Lavinia were both enrolled at Amherst Academy, a converted boys' school with progressive educational ideals; here they studied subjects such as botany, chemistry, languages, and art, and attended lectures by visiting academics. By all accounts Dickinson was an engaged scholar, respected for her sense of humor and the strength of her intellect; she was also passionate about music and enjoyed dancing. In 1847, she began her secondary education at Mount Holyoke Female Seminary, where there was more emphasis on religious faith. Dickinson, who had not been baptized and who even at a young age maintained her distance from the established Puritanism of her community, publicly upheld her nonconformity. A fellow student, Clara Turner, remembered a day when the director of the school "asked all those who wanted to be Christians to rise." Dickinson remained in her seat and said to Clara: "They thought it queer I didn't rise—I thought a lie would be queerer." For reasons that remain somewhat unclear but that likely had to do with ill health, Dickinson left Mount Holyoke after a year, returning home in 1848.

In her time at school, Dickinson had developed several significant and intense friendships with both men and women. While at Amherst Academy, she became close to Leonard Humphrey, the principal of the school, who nurtured her love of reading. He was the first of a series of older male friends that Dickinson would refer to variously as "Tutor" or "Preceptor." The second was an attorney, Benjamin Franklin Newton, who worked with her father, and who introduced her to the works of William Wordsworth, Henry Wadsworth Longfellow, Ralph Waldo Emerson, and Lydia Maria Child. In the late 1840s, Dickinson met Susan Gilbert (later Susan Gilbert Dickinson), who was to become a life-long friend and eventually sister-in-law; the two formed a close bond and carried on a passionate correspondence; their letters have been interpreted by some later scholars as evidence of a romantic relationship. Dickinson wrote at least ninety-four poems to Susan, who— intelligent, sensitive, and open-minded—became very dear to the poet.

Dickinson's early life was also repeatedly marked by tragic loss. Her cousin and friend, Sophia Holland, died of typhus fever in 1844, and Dickinson's grief and ensuing depression were so deep that she was sent to Boston to recover. In May 1848, another friend, Jacob Holt, died, and two years later, Leonard Humphrey died of a brain aneurysm at the age of twenty-five. Three years later, Benjamin Newton died of tuberculosis when he was thirty-two. These were deep emotional blows to Dickinson, whose sensibility was marked by this series of young deaths; her poetry returns again and again to the themes of death, loss, and separation: "Parting is all we know of heaven / And all we need of hell."

When Dickinson returned home from school, she felt acutely the contrast between the relative freedom of school life and the constrictions of a home life in which a young woman was expected to devote her time to domestic duties. As she wrote to her friend Abiah Root in 1850, "God keep me from what they call households." Dickinson nonetheless took on many of these duties—and continued to do so throughout her life. She was a dedicated and gifted gardener; she baked the family desserts and bread; and she took care of her often-ailing mother. Dickinson also took steps, however, to secure some hours to herself, and she began in 1849 to write poetry. She refused to accept many of the social demands typically placed on the women of a prominent family like hers, withdrawing from the custom of "visiting" and receiving visitors; she saw only her family and closest friends.

Her need to preserve freedom may also have had a good deal to do with her decision not to marry. She wrote to Susan in 1852 about the merits of a single life: "How dull our lives must seem to the bride, and the plighted maiden, whose days are fed with gold, and who gathers pearls every evening; but to the *wife*, Susie, sometimes the *wife forgotten*, our lives perhaps seem dearer than all others in the world." Dickinson's choice to remain single did not mean that she lived without passionate attachments, however. She had intense relationships with both men and women throughout her life, mainly carried on through written correspondence (with the Reverend Charles Wadsworth, Benjamin Newton, and Susan Dickinson, among others). It is not clear to what degree these relationships were sexual, but it is abundantly clear that they could be passionate—and that, as the poet Adrienne Rich put it, Dickinson "was attracted by and interested in" men and women "whose minds had something to offer her."

In 1850 the Great Revival swept through Amherst, and Dickinson's father, sister, and many of her friends joined the local Congregationalist Church and declared themselves "for Christ." Dickinson did not join the church, as she had trouble accepting some of the tenets of the Congregationalist faith—particularly those surrounding predestination and hell. As she began to write more and more poetry, Dickinson often voiced religious concerns, but her spirituality was individual; she refused to adhere to a prescribed form of Christianity. In a letter to Jane Humphrey in 1850, she wrote: "Christ is calling everyone here, all my companions have answered … and I am standing alone in rebellion, and growing very careless. … I can't tell you *what* they have found, but *they* think it is something precious. I wonder if it *is*?"

At the Homestead, Dickinson continued to read widely in British and American literature, particularly the novelists and poets of her own century. She was also fond of the early modern poets—especially of William Shakespeare, of whose works she wrote to a friend, "Why is any other book needed?" Dickinson's own verse carries echoes of all these sources—as well as of the King James Bible, to whose rhetorical structures and poetic language she had been thoroughly introduced as a child.

However much she drew on literary traditions, Dickinson's own use of language, and the poetic forms she shaped, are unique. Most of her poetry is loosely organized according to stanzaic and metrical forms commonly used in Christian hymns—forms with relatively short rhymed lines, typically grouped in four-line stanzas. But Dickinson experiments with and transforms these traditional structures, using enjambment, imperfect and suspended rhymes, iconoclastic punctuation, and unusual word order to disrupt expectations and present compressed thoughts and feelings in extraordinarily suggestive ways.

Over the course of the 1850s the group of friends with whom Dickinson corresponded grew into something of a literary network. During her lifetime this was the primary audience for her poems, a quarter of which she sent to her friends in letters—letters which often also included reflections in prose that could be almost as cryptically expressive and fascinating as the poems themselves. "A letter," she wrote, "always feels to me like immortality because it is the mind alone without corporeal friend."

In the 1850s, Dickinson began to write to several correspondents from the literary world; these included two editors of the abolitionist newspaper *Springfield Republican*, Samuel Bowles and Josiah Holland. Bowles published seven of her lyrics in his paper, smoothing out a good deal of what he saw as Dickinson's idiosyncratic punctuation, rhymes, line breaks, and rhythms—a practice her other early editors also followed. Dickinson does not appear to have made any attempt to prevent such publication, and there is evidence in her letters with Susan that the two young women were looking forward to seeing "Safe in their Alabaster Chambers" in print. In other letters and poems, however, such as "A Narrow fellow in the Grass" (1863) and "Publication – is the Auction" (1865), the speaker expresses highly ambivalent views toward the ideas of publicity and fame.

Dickinson's most prolific period of writing began in the late 1850s and continued to the mid-1860s, by which time she had written over a thousand poems. In 1858, she began making fair copies, organizing the poems into groups later called "fascicles," which she sewed together by hand. In the spring of 1862, Dickinson read an article in *The Atlantic Monthly* by the literary critic Thomas Wentworth Higginson. Wanting an educated opinion on her work, she sent him four poems, asking if her poetry "breathed." This letter prompted the beginning of a correspondence with Higginson that would last until Dickinson's death. Though he offered her some criticism and some poetic advice, Higginson greatly admired the poetry and was sensitive to the power of her personality; he became a great support to her (she later told him that he had saved her life by responding to her query). Though she wrote to him in the language of a student to her teacher, she maintained a confident independence about her work; rarely if ever did she take his advice. For his part, Higginson may have suggested regularizing a good deal of her grammar and punctuation, but he described her poetry as "woven out of the heart's own atoms," and later acknowledged that "when a thought takes one's breath away, a lesson in grammar seems an impertinence."

In the early 1860s, Dickinson's reclusiveness increased, as did her creativity and poetic output. Her poems became even more experimental and dynamic, and she began increasingly to add variants to her manuscripts—alternative word choices that she wrote down in footnotes or in marginalia, allowing for at times radically different readings to coexist within a given poem. Scholars have noted that her most productive period coincided with the Civil War. She wrote in a letter that "Sorrow seems more general than it did, and not the estate of a few persons, since the war began; and if the anguish of others helped one with one's own, now would be many medicines. …"

The loss of Dickinson's father in 1874 caused prolonged grief, as her letters attest. "I dream about father every night," she wrote, "always a different dream, and forget what I am doing daytimes, wondering where he is. Without any body, I keep thinking. What kind can that be?" Her mother had a stroke the following year and broke her hip, and Dickinson became the primary caregiver until her mother's death in 1882. After a period of increasing ill health, Dickinson herself died on 15 May 1886, of kidney disease; she was buried beside her parents in Amherst.

The story of how the bulk of Dickinson's poems first saw publication after her death is complicated by a family disagreement. It began with the arrival in Amherst of David Todd, an astronomy professor, and his talented wife, Mabel Loomis Todd, in 1881. Dickinson's brother Austin and his wife, Susan Dickinson, both befriended Mabel. Dickinson also took an interest in her, albeit from afar: she would listen to Mabel sing and speak to her through a door, but the two never met. (Mabel, however, took a deep interest in Dickinson, and felt assured of her poetic genius.) The web of friendship frayed, however, when Austin and Mabel fell in love; the two began an affair that lasted for the remainder of Austin's life. After Dickinson's death, her sister Lavinia found a large cache of poems in Emily's chest of drawers; Lavinia eventually gave these to Mabel Todd to prepare for publication. Susan Dickinson, meanwhile, had a separate collection of poems and letters that Emily had given her over the course of their lifetime of friendship. The ensuing feud between Susan and Mabel over Dickinson's legacy continued down through their daughters' generation.

Mabel Todd, together with Higginson, edited the first two editions of Dickinson's verse, *Poems* (1890) and *Poems* (1891); these editions did not include any of the material from Susan Dickinson's collection. Todd and Higginson added titles to the poems, grouped them thematically—Dickinson did not title or number her work—and standardized much of her grammar and punctuation, with the intent of making the poetry more accessible. Their interventions received considerable censure in the late twentieth and early twenty-first centuries; the uncomplicated view that Helen McNeil expressed in the introduction to her 1986 edition—that Dickinson's "works were mangled by editors"—was widely shared. More recent scholarship has been less censorious and more alive to historical context—alive both to the extent that Dickinson's approach to poetry was ahead of her time, and to the sort of reception that her work would likely have received in the late nineteenth century had it been published with her manuscript capitalization, punctuation, and grammar intact. Even in Todd and Higginson's "cleaned up" versions, Dickinson's style met with a hostile reception from not a few critics; the reviewer for the popular *Scribner's Monthly*, for example, complained of her "neglect of form" and her "perverseness and eccentricity," while the famous British critic Andrew Lang was more caustic, writing in the *Daily News* that Dickinson "reminds us of no sane nor educated writer." Other critics were far more positive, however. The reviewer for the *New York Commercial Advertiser* termed Dickinson "the poet in quintessence," and in *Harper's*, William Dean Howells (perhaps the leading American arbiter of literary taste during the period) praised her "short, quick impulses of intense feeling or poignant thought," and concluded that her "strange poetry" constituted "a distinctive addition to the literature of the world." The poems were popular with the public as well—particularly among female readers; eleven editions were issued by the end of 1892.

After Susan Dickinson's death, her daughter, Martha Dickinson Bianchi, decided to publish the Dickinson poems and letters that had been in her mother's possession, under the title *The Single Hound* (1914). This volume sparked another surge of interest in Dickinson's poetry, one that launched her as a proto-modernist. In a review of *The Single Hound*, Harriet Monroe called Dickinson "an unconscious and uncatalogued Imagiste." This marked a moment in the history of Dickinson criticism when scholars began situating the poet within larger intellectual contexts—in relation not only to New England Transcendentalism and Puritanism, but also to international movements such as Imagism, the early twentieth-century literary movement that valued concision, clarity, and formal experimentation. Modernist critics also placed Dickinson within the tradition of seventeenth-century Metaphysical poets such as Henry Vaughan and John Donne. By the early 1920s, Dickinson was firmly established as a significant American poet. In Conrad Aiken's introduction to *Selected Poems of Emily Dickinson* (1924), he describes her poetry as "perhaps the finest, by a woman, in the English language." Interestingly, however, Dickinson remained marginalized in many conventional narratives of the development of American literature; neither the 1924 *Short History of American Literature* nor the 1925 *Literary History of America* include any mention of her at all.

In 1955, the scholar Thomas H. Johnson collected all the Dickinson poems and letters that were, at that time, known to exist; his edition presented the poems for the first time in an approximation of their original state, and in an attempt at chronological order. Johnson's edition sparked renewed interest in her poetry—and that interest has never let up in the intervening decades. Scholars in the 1960s focused largely on thematic and linguistic concerns, those in the 1970s largely on feminist and psychoanalytic readings. Scholars continued as well to research her life and build her biography, as well as to consider her within wider nineteenth-century contexts. In 1998 came another major editorial achievement, Ralph Franklin's edition of the poems, which offered a more reliable order and chronology than had that of Johnson (Franklin was able to trace, from watermarks and pinholes, the original order of poems in Dickinson's fascicles). In 2013, the online open-access Emily Dickinson Archive was launched, allowing all interested readers and scholars to engage with images of the manuscripts. And in 2016, Cristanne Miller published a ground-breaking new edition, *Emily Dickinson's Poems: As She Preserved Them*, presenting all the poems in Dickinson's canon as they were copied down—those that were sewn into her forty fascicles, and those that she had kept in draft form.

In the twenty-first century, critical approaches to Dickinson have emphasized the materiality of her manuscripts and probed into the history of her various editors, with a focus on gender politics. Critics have also been considering Dickinson's poetry from the perspectives of ecocriticism, animal studies, queer theory, disability studies, race studies, and digital humanities. Dickinson's influence on American and world literatures has been profound. Readers, poets, and critics alike return to Dickinson for her ability to push the boundaries of language and poetic form, and for her articulation of a vision of human experience that is unique in its suggestive power, its compressed emotion, and its ability to prompt questions. As Dickinson biographer Richard B. Sewall has put it, "We still are not quite sure of her. We ask and ask."

NOTE ON THE TEXTS: It is by this time a commonplace to acknowledge that Dickinson's style is sufficiently idiosyncratic as to make it entirely appropriate for editors to treat her as a special case. For obvious reasons, we have suspended some of *The Broadview Anthology of American Literature*'s usual conventions—most notably, our usual practice of modernizing or regularizing punctuation and capitalization. We have also suspended our usual conventions regarding the dating of works; our normal practice is to foreground the date of first publication of each work; in Dickinson's case it is for obvious reasons the date of composition that appears after each poem.

The texts printed in these pages are based on the handwritten manuscripts themselves, in the facsimile form in which the Emily Dickinson Archive, in cooperation with the Houghton Library at Harvard University (and other institutions holding the manuscripts), now makes the vast majority of Dickinson's manuscript versions available to the general public. (Like all editors—and all readers of Dickinson—we are greatly in their debt for the opportunity to experience her manuscripts directly.)

In preparing the texts of the poems included in this volume we have also consulted the three major editions that are based directly on the manuscripts: Thomas H. Johnson's *The Complete Poems of Emily Dickinson* (1955); R.W. Franklin's *The Poems of Emily Dickinson* (1998); and Cristanne Miller's *Emily Dickinson's Poems: As She Preserved Them* (2016). In many cases where the transcriptions of these editors differ from one another, we provide information in the notes as to those differences, often indicating our reasoning in siding with one editor over another or—in a very few cases—in offering a reading different from those of any of the three.

We also in these pages provide examples of the manuscripts themselves in facsimile form. As those examples show very clearly, *any* transcription of Dickinson's poems into a printed form entails judgment calls as to what constitutes a dash and what a period; as to whether or not a letter is capitalized; as to where line breaks occur, and so on. Following Johnson, Franklin, and Miller, we standardize all marks perceived to be dashes (Johnson standardizes using an em dash; we, like Franklin and Miller, employ a spaced en dash). But as all editors acknowledge—and as anyone reading the manuscripts for themselves can plainly see—those marks in a substantial number of poems[1] vary very widely indeed. Some are high in the line, some in the middle, some well below the line; some are very long and emphatically rendered, others are as short as to make it difficult to be sure if they are intended as dashes or as periods. A great many marks—especially at the ends of lines—have a downwards left to right slant to them, and are distinctly below the line. Miller conjectures that, "like many of her contemporaries, [Dickinson] probably quite often wrote elongated periods—in a kind of rolling stop. She may also have written commas both high within her row of script and slanting right rather than left." Miller nevertheless decides not to "thoroughly revise earlier interpretations of these marks." Such decisions are entirely defensible; they have the merit of simplicity, and do not risk confusing readers who have, over the decades since the publication of Johnson's edition, become familiar with the convention of representing a wide variety of Dickinson's marks in the same way. (For that very reason we have maintained the "one-size dash" convention in the transcriptions found in these pages.) But such decisions implicitly concede that print transcriptions of Dickinson's handwritten manuscripts inevitably entail a good deal of interpretation. The reality is that it is simply not known, for example, whether Dickinson intended a mark that resembles a right-slanting comma to be read as some form of dash, as a comma, or as a mark with some other, special meaning. In recognition of these realities, we have also, in the case of a small number of the poems included in these pages, presented alternative transcriptions alongside the conventional ones.

In the case of several poems, we have also provided examples of early editing practice; this edition's two-column format allows us conveniently to place different versions side by side, providing a convenient portfolio for the purposes of comparison.

In these pages we order the poems chronologically, taking the lead of Johnson and Franklin (and drawing as well on the scholarship of Miller). As one other part of this volume, however, we present one complete fascicle—Fascicle 13—for the benefit of those who wish to study a group of Dickinson's poems "as she preserved them," to use Miller's phrase. Miller's edition has many merits, not the least of which is the degree to which it encourages scholars, students, and readers generally, to think of Dickinson afresh; we hope that the various ways in which Dickinson is presented in these pages will, in much more modest fashion, serve a similar end.

⌘ ⌘ ⌘

---

[1] Much as the transcription issues are of considerable interest and real significance, it is important too to make clear that they are not ubiquitous. A poem such as "These are the days when Birds come back" is in this respect not typical. Indeed, a great many of Dickinson's poems present few transcription issues, or none at all; all editors are in agreement as to what is capitalized, what is a dash and what is a comma, etc.

SELECTED POEMS

[*It's all I have to bring today —*][1]

It's all I have to bring today –
This, and my heart beside –
This, and my heart, and all the fields –
And all the meadows wide –
5   Be sure you count – sh'd I forget
Some one the sum could tell[2] –
This, and my heart, and all the Bees
Which in the Clover dwell.
        —1858

[*I never lost as much but twice —*][3]

I never lost as much but[4] twice –
And that was in the sod.
Twice have I stood a beggar
Before the door of God!

5   Angels – twice descending
Reimbursed my store –
Burglar! Banker – Father!
I am poor once more!
        —1858

[*I robbed the woods —*][5]

I robbed the Woods –
The trusting Woods –
The unsuspecting Trees
Brought out their
5   Burs[6] and mosses
My fantasy to please.
I scanned their trinkets curious –
I grasped – I bore away –
What will the solemn Hemlock[7] –
10 What will the Oak tree say?
        —1859

---

1   This poem appears in Johnson as Poem 26; in Franklin as Poem 17; and in Miller as the second poem in Sheet 3 of Fascicle 1, page 38. The present text is in complete accord with the transcriptions of Franklin and Miller; the marks after "fields" and after "count," however, could plausibly be transcribed as right-slanting commas.

2   *the sum could tell*   I.e., it would be reflected in the total number.

3   This poem appears in Johnson as Poem 49; in Franklin as Poem 39; and in Miller as the second poem in Sheet 3 of Fascicle 3, page 57. There are no transcription issues.

It is worth noting that Sheets 3 and 4 of this fascicle are made up of poems composed in 1858, whereas the fascicle's first two sheets are made up of poems dating from 1859.

4   *but*   Except.

5   This poem appears in Johnson as Poem 41; in Franklin as Poem 57; and in Miller as the fourth poem in Sheet 3 of Fascicle 2, page 47. The present text is in agreement with Johnson in reading the mark at the end of the sixth line as a period, but in agreement with Franklin and Miller in reading the mark at the end of line 2 as a dash. The marks at the ends of lines 7, 8, and 9 could all plausibly be transcribed as right-slanting commas. A facsimile of the manuscript appears overleaf.

6   *Burs*   Acorns from the bur oak tree.

7   *Hemlock*   The reference is to the North American hemlock pine, not to the poisonous plant of the same name.

80-4

X I

I robbed the Woods.
The trusting Woods.
The unsuspecting Trees
Brought out their Burs and mosses
My fantasy to please.
I scanned their trinkets curious
I grasped - I bore away.
What will the solemn Hemlock.
What will the Oak tree say?

A Leaf! Help's! Help's!
Another Leaf!
Four Prayers. Oh Passer by!
From such a Common Ball as this
Might date a Victory!
From marshallings as simple
The flags of nations swang.
Steady - my soul! What issues
Upon thine arrow hang!

[*Success is counted sweetest*][1]

Success is counted sweetest
By those who ne'er succeed.
To comprehend a nectar
Requires sorest need.

5   Not one of all the purple Host
Who took the Flag[2] today
Can tell the definition
So clear of Victory

As he defeated – dying –
10 On whose forbidden ear
The distant strains of triumph
Burst agonized and clear!
—1859

SUCCESS.

SUCCESS is counted sweetest
By those who ne'er succeed.
To comprehend a Nectar
Requires the sorest need.
Not one of all the Purple Host
Who took the flag to-day,
Can tell the definition,
So plain, of Victory,
As he defeated, dying,
On whose forbidden ear
The distant strains of triumph
Break, agonizing clear.

---

[1]   This poem appears in Johnson as Poem 67; in Franklin as Poem
112; and in Miller as the third poem in Sheet 1 of Fascicle 5, page 69.
The present transcription is in complete agreement with those of all
three of these editors. The fascicle version probably dates from the
summer of 1859; variant manuscript versions (in which the poem
is not divided into stanzas) were sent to Susan Dickinson in 1859
and to Thomas Wentworth Higginson in July of 1862. The poem
was first published in the *Brooklyn Daily Union*, 27 April 1862; that
version (the source of which is presumed to have been a now-lost
manuscript copy) was reprinted in 1878 in the anthology *A Masque
of Poets*. Higginson and Todd made slight revisions for *Poems* (1890);
this is the poem that opens that volume.

[2]   *took the Flag*   Won the battle.

[These are the days when Birds come back ˏ][1]

[These are the days when Birds come back ˏ]

These are the days when Birds come back ˏ
A very few – a Bird or two ˏ
To take a backward look.

These are the days when skies resume
5   The old . old sophistries[2] of June ˏ
A blue and gold mistake.

Oh fraud that cannot cheat the Bee.
Almost thy plausibility
Induces my belief,

10   Till ranks of seeds their witness bear –
And softly thro' the altered air
Hurries a timid leaf.

Oh sacrament of summer days,
Oh Last Communion[3] in the Haze ˏ
15   Permit a child to join,

Thy sacred emblems to partake ˏ
Thy consecrated bread to take
And thine immortal wine!
—1859

1   This poem appears in Johnson as Poem 130; in Franklin as Poem 122; and in Miller as the first poem in Sheet 3 of Fascicle 6, pages 81–82. The fascicle manuscript is the only manuscript version extant.

This poem is a good example of how difficult it is to transcribe Dickinson's manuscript writings into print with complete confidence. Karen Dandurand (the scholar who, in the 1980s, discovered that three poems had been published in *Drum Beat* in the 1860s) has fairly suggested of this poem that "most of the marks rendered by Johnson as dashes look as much, or more, like commas angled downward to the right, or like indeterminate dots." But subsequent editors have in this case followed Johnson; Franklin and Miller diverge from Johnson only in how they reproduce the mark at the end of one line ("Permit a child to join"), which Johnson prints as a period, Franklin prints as a dash, and Miller prints as a comma.

A facsimile of the first page of the 1859 manuscript version appears above and also (in larger format) on page 14. In the next column we offer a transcription that endeavors to present the marks more-or-less as they appear in the manuscript. In the third column a conventional transcription is provided, with the right-slanting marks interpreted as dashes. The fourth column prints the text as it was published (from a now-lost manuscript) in *Drum Beat*, 11 March 1864.

A version of the poem was included in Todd and Higginson's *Poems* (1890) under the title "Indian Summer."

2   *sophistries*   Deceptive reasonings.

3   *Last Communion*   Christian sacrament administered to the dying; the recipient eats bread and drinks wine in remembrance of Christ's sacrifice. The ritual is thought to bind the departing soul with Christ and thus with the promise of eternal life.

[These are the days when Birds come back —]

These are the days when Birds come back –
A very few – a Bird or two –
To take a backward look.

These are the days when skies resume
5   The old – old sophistries of June –
A blue and gold mistake.

Oh fraud that cannot cheat the Bee,
Almost thy plausibility
Induces my belief,

10   Till ranks of seeds their witness bear –
And softly thro' the altered air
Hurries a timid leaf.

Oh sacrament of summer days,
Oh Last Communion in the Haze –
15   Permit a child to join

Thy sacred emblems to partake –
Thy consecrated bread to take
And thine immortal wine!
　　—1859

[October]

These are the days when birds come back,
A very few, a bird or two,
To take a backward look.

These are the days when skies resume
5   The old, old sophistries of June,—
A blue and gold mistake.

Oh, fraud that cannot cheat the bee!
Almost thy plausibility
Induces my belief,

10   Till ranks of seeds their witness bear,
And softly, through the altered air,
Hurries a timid leaf.

Oh, sacrament of summer days,
Oh last communion in the haze,
15   Permit a child to join!

Thy sacred emblems to partake,
Thy consecrated bread to take,
And thine immortal wine!
　　—1864

XXſ

These are the days when Birds come back.
A very few - a Bird or two.
to take a backward look.

These are the days when Skies resume
the old. old sophistries of June.
a blue and gold mistake.

Oh fraud that cannot cheat the Bee.
Almost thy plausibility -
Induces my belief.

Till ranks of seeds their witness bear.
And softly thro the altered air
Hurries a timid leaf.

Oh Sacrament of summer days.
Oh Last Communion in the Haze.
Permit a Child to join.

Perhaps a squirrel may remain.
My sentiments to share.
Grant me, Oh Lord, a sunny mind,
Thy windy will to bear!

Safe in their Alabaster Chambers,
Untouched by morning
And untouched by noon
Sleep the meek members of the Resurrection
Rafter of Satin,
And roof of Stone.

Light laughs the Breeze
In her Castle above them.
Babbles the Bee in a stolid Ear,
Pipe the Sweet Birds in ignorant Cadence
Ah, what sagacity perished here!

[*Safe in their Alabaster Chambers* –][1]

Safe in their Alabaster[2] Chambers –
Untouched by Morning
And untouched by Noon –
Sleep the meek members of the Resurrection[3] –
5 Rafter of satin,
And Roof of stone.

Light laughs the breeze
In her Castle above them –
Babbles the Bee in a stolid Ear,
10 Pipe the Sweet Birds in ignorant cadence –
Ah, what sagacity perished here!
—1859 VERSION

[*Safe in their Alabaster Chambers,*][4]

Safe in their Alabaster Chambers,
Untouched by Morning –
And untouched by Noon –
Lie the meek members of the Resurrection –
5 Rafter of Satin and Roof of Stone –

Grand go the Years – in the Crescent – above them –
Worlds scoop their Arcs –
And Firmaments – row –
Diadems – drop – and Doges[5] – surrender –
10 Soundless as dots – on a Disc of snow –
—1861 VERSION

---

[1] (See also the previous page.) This poem appears in Johnson as Poem 216; in Franklin as Poem 124; and in Miller as the third poem in Sheet 3 of Fascicle 6, page 83 [the 1859 version] and also as the third poem in Sheet 4 of Fascicle 10, page 122 [the 1861 version]. The present transcription is in agreement with those of Franklin and Miller—though it is worth noting that the marks at the ends of lines 1, 3, and 4 may plausibly be read as right-slanting commas rather than dashes.

A variant of this 1859 version was published (with the title "The Sleeping") in the *Springfield Republican*, 1 March 1862.

[2] *Alabaster* Smooth, translucent white stone, frequently used for carving and statuary.

[3] *members of the Resurrection* I.e., the dead; those awaiting Judgment Day and the resurrection of the body.

[4] This 1861 version of the poem appears in Johnson as a variant of Poem 216; in Franklin as a variant of Poem 124; and in Miller as the third poem in Sheet 4 of Fascicle 10, page 122. The present transcription of the 1861 fascicle manuscript is in agreement with those of Franklin and Miller, except in two particulars: with Franklin, we read "Chambers" in line 1 as upper case; and, with Miller, we read "Noon" in line 3 as upper case. (Both can plausibly be read either way.)

An additional 1861 trial version of the second stanza may be found on page 81 of this edition, in an 1861 letter from Dickinson to Susan Gilbert Dickinson.

[5] *Doges* Magistrates holding high civil office in the Venetian Republic from the seventh to the eighteenth centuries; the republic of Genoa also had a similar office.

[Besides the Autumn poets sing][1]

Besides[2] the Autumn poets sing
A few prosaic days
A little this side of the snow
And that side of the Haze.

5 A few incisive mornings –
A few Ascetic[3] eves –
Gone – Mr Bryant's "Golden Rod" –
And Mr Thomson's "sheaves."[4]

Still, is the bustle in the Brook –
10 Sealed are the spicy valves[5] –
Mesmeric fingers softly touch
The eyes of many Elves –

Perhaps a squirrel may remain –
My sentiments to share –
15 Grant me, Oh Lord, a sunny mind –
Thy windy will to bear!
—1859

[All overgrown by cunning moss,][6]

All overgrown by cunning[7] moss,
All interspersed with – weed,
The little cage of "Currer Bell"
In quiet "Haworth"[8] laid.

5 This Bird – observing others
When frosts too sharp became
Retire to other latitudes –
Quietly did the same –

But differed in returning –
10 Since Yorkshire hills are green –
Yet not in all the nests I meet –
Can Nightingale[9] be seen –

Or –

Gathered from many wanderings
15 Gethsemane[10] can tell

---

[1] This poem appears in Johnson as Poem 131; in Franklin as Poem 123; and in Miller as the second poem in Sheet 3 of Fascicle 6, page 82. The present transcription has been made according to conventional principles and, except for reading the mark after "Haze" as a period, is in accord with those of Johnson, Franklin, and Miller (all of whom print the poem with a dash after "Gone" in line 7, and with dashes at the ends of lines 5, 6, 7, 9, 10, 13, 14, and 15). These marks could all plausibly be read differently, however—the mark after "Gone" as a period; and the other marks as right-slanting commas. An alternative transcription appears in the website component of this anthology.

The poem appears in Todd and Higginson's *Poems* (1891) as Poem 49; they assign to it the title "November."

[2] *Besides* In addition to, beyond.

[3] *Ascetic* Austere, self-denying; Christian Ascetics withdrew from society and practiced abstinence and fasting, adhering to rigorous schedules of work and prayer.

[4] *Mr Bryant's "Golden Rod"* See "The Death of the Flowers," line 15, by American poet William Cullen Bryant (1794–1878); *Mr Thomson's "sheaves"* See "Autumn," a section of the longer work *The Seasons*, by Scottish poet James Thomson (1700–48), lines 168 and 180.

[5] *spicy valves* I.e., flowers or seed pods that open or split like valves or doors; may refer more specifically to the "valves" of the flower's nectaries (which release scent as well as nectar).

[6] This poem appears in Johnson as Poem 148; in Franklin as Poem 146; and in Miller as the second poem in Sheet 1, Fascicle 7, pages 86–87. The poem exists in only one manuscript version; at the end of the third stanza Dickinson writes "Or –" on a separate line, and then provides two more stanzas as alternatives. The poem is thus frequently printed including only the first three stanzas—although some editions have printed it as a three-stanza poem with Dickinson's alternative stanzas substituted for stanzas 2 and 3.

The transcription provided here is in agreement with those of Franklin and Miller except in one particular; the present editors read the mark between "with" and "weed" in line 2 as a dash, whereas Franklin and Miller have presumably read the mark between the two words as the cross from the "t" in "with." Dickinson certainly often places the crosses for her "t"s well beyond where the letter itself appears, but rarely so far forward as here—and rarely so low.

[7] *cunning* Skillful and crafty, as well as quaint, attractive.

[8] *Currer Bell* Pseudonym of English novelist and poet Charlotte Brontë (1816–55); *Haworth* Name of the parsonage where the Brontë family lived in Yorkshire, England (the graveyard attached to the church was directly adjacent to the parsonage house).

[9] *Nightingale* Migratory thrush whose beautiful, haunting song and habit of night-time singing have led to a symbolic association with poets and singers.

[10] *Gethsemane* Garden in Jerusalem where Christ prayed and endured agony of mind before his arrest and crucifixion.

Thro' what transporting anguish
She reached the Asphodel![1]

Soft fall the sounds of Eden
Upon her puzzled ear –
20 Oh what an afternoon for Heaven,
When "Bronte" entered there!
—1860

[I'm "wife" – I've finished that –][2]

I'm "wife" – I've finished that –
That other state –
I'm Czar[3] – I'm "Woman" now –
It's safer so –

5   How odd the Girl's life looks
Behind this soft Eclipse –
I think that Earth feels so
To folks in Heaven – now –

This being comfort – then
10 That other kind – was pain –
But why compare?
I'm "Wife"! Stop there!
—1861

[Title divine – is mine!][4]

Title divine – is mine!
The Wife – without the Sign!
Acute Degree – conferred on me –
Empress of Calvary![5]
5   Royal – all but the Crown!
Betrothed – without the swoon
God sends us Women –
When you – hold – Garnet to Garnet –
Gold – to Gold –
10 Born – Bridalled[6] – Shrouded –
In a Day –
Tri Victory
"My Husband" – women say –
Stroking the Melody –
15 Is this – the way?
—c. 1861

---

[4] This poem appears in Johnson as Poem 1072; in Franklin as
Poem 194; and in Miller under "Poems Not Retained" on page 701.
The poem exists in two manuscript versions (one to Samuel Bowles,
the other to Susan Dickinson), both sent by Dickinson as letters, and
both including this message following the poem itself: "Here's what I
had to 'tell you' –you will tell no other: – Honor – is its own pawn."
(Dickinson uses the "Honor is its own pawn" appeal in her 16 April
1862 letter to Thomas Wentworth Higginson.)

    One line appears only in the version sent to Susan Dickinson;
the Bowles version does not include the line "Tri Victory." In the
Bowles version (but not in the Susan Dickinson) the word "this"
in the final line is underlined. The present transcription is from the
Susan Dickinson letter; Miller transcribes from the Bowles letter,
while both Johnson (in *Final Harvest*) and Franklin (in *The Poems of
Emily Dickinson: Reading Edition*) offer a composite version, includ-
ing the "Tri Victory" line from the Susan Dickinson version and the
underlining of "this" from the Bowles version.

    Further alternative transcriptions of this poem are certainly
conceivable, given that many of the marks which have traditionally
been read as dashes take a form more suggestive of right-slanting
commas.

[5] *Calvary* Place where Christ was crucified.

[6] *Bridalled* I.e., married (with a pun on "bridled").

---

[1] *Asphodel* In Greek mythology, this white flower covers the
Elysian Fields, where heroes and virtuous souls rested after death.

[2] This poem appears in Johnson as Poem 199; in Franklin as Poem
225; and in Miller as the fourth poem in Sheet 6, Fascicle 9, pages
112–13. There are few transcription issues—though the "dash" follow-
ing "kind" in line 10 arguably might be better represented by a dot
than a line of any length.

    Todd and Higginson included the poem under the title
"Apocalypse" in their edition of *Poems* (1890); aside from differences
in punctuation, the version there includes two word changes in the
second stanza; "feels" to "seems" and "folks" to "those."

[3] *Czar* Title of the emperor of Russia.

[*Faith is a fine invention*][1]

Faith is a fine invention
For Gentlemen who *see*.
But *Microscopes* are prudent
In an Emergency!
—1861

[*"Faith" is a fine invention*]

"Faith" is a fine invention
For Gentlemen who <u>see</u>!
But Microscopes are prudent
In an Emergency!
—1861

[*Some keep the Sabbath going to Church —*][2]

Some keep the Sabbath going to Church –
I keep it, staying at Home –
With a Bobolink[3] for a Chorister –
And an Orchard, for a Dome –

5 Some keep the Sabbath in Surplice[4] –
I just wear my Wings –
And instead of tolling the Bell, for Church,
Our little Sexton[5] – sings.

God preaches, a noted Clergyman –
10 And the sermon is never long,
So instead of getting to Heaven, at last –
I'm going, all along.
—1861

---

[1] The earliest extant version of this poem is that which appears in a letter to Samuel Bowles (dating probably from late 1860 or early 1861):

Dear Mr Bowles
Thank you.
    "Faith" is a fine invention
    When Gentlemen can see –
    But Microscopes are prudent
    In an Emergency.
You spoke of the "East." I have thought about it this winter.
    Don't you think you and I should be shrewder, to take the <u>Mountain Road</u>?
    That <u>Bareheaded life</u> – under the grass – worries one like a wasp.
    The Rose is for Mary.
        Emily.

Dickinson included a revised version of the poem in Fascicle 10 (printed first above), and included a slightly different version in Fascicle 12 the next year (also printed above). The standard editions take different approaches to the poem: Johnson prints a transcription of the 1860 Bowles letter version as Poem 185; Franklin prints a transcription of the Fascicle 12 version as Poem 202; and Miller prints both fascicle versions (Fascicle 10, Sheet 1, page 119; Fascicle 12, Sheet 1, page 137), while noting in a footnote the existence of the Bowles letter version. Miller reads the punctuation at the end of the second line of the Fascicle 10 version as a dash; in other respects the present transcriptions are in accord with hers.

[2] This poem appears in Johnson as Poem 324; in Franklin as Poem 236; and in Miller as the final poem of Fascicle 9, Sheet 7, page 115. In their one-volume editions, both Johnson and Franklin print the version that Dickinson sent to Thomas Wentworth Higginson in July of 1861; that version is also used as the base text here. Miller prints the fascicle version (believed to date from the spring of 1861).

    The poem was published (from a now-lost manuscript copy) in *Round Table*, 12 March 1864, under the title "My Sabbath," and was published by Todd and Higginson in *Poems* (1890) under the title "A Service of Song." As was standard practice when Dickinson's poems were published in her lifetime, capitalization, and punctuation were regularized; this resulted in the removal of most of the dashes—but also in the addition of one dash (both the *Round Table* version and the *Poems* [1890] version add a comma after "preaches" in line 9).

    Further alternative transcriptions of this poem are certainly conceivable, given that many of the marks which have traditionally been read as dashes take a form more suggestive of right-slanting commas; the "dashes" at the ends of lines 2, 3, and 6 take this form, and the mark after "Heaven" is represented as a dot in the middle of the line rather than a comma, or, as it is sometimes transcribed, a dash.

[3] *Bobolink* North American songbird with a cheerful, tinkling song; its black and white plumage gives the bird a clerical look.

[4] *Surplice* Type of vestment worn by ministers, choristers, and other church officials.

[5] *Sexton* Caretaker of a church who traditionally rang the church bells.

[*The Lamp burns sure – within –*][1]

The Lamp burns sure – within –
Tho' Serfs[2] – supply the Oil –
It matters not the busy Wick –
At her phosphoric[3] toil!

5   The Slave – forgets – to fill –
The Lamp – burns golden – on –
Unconscious that the oil is out –
As that the Slave – is gone.
—1861

[*I came to buy a smile – today –*][4]

I came to buy a smile – today –
But just a single smile –
The smallest one upon your cheek
Will suit me just as well –
5   The one that no one else would miss
It shone so very small –
I'm pleading at the counter – sir –
Could you afford to sell?

I've Diamonds – on my fingers –
10   You know what Diamonds are!
I've Rubies – like the Evening Blood –
And Topaz – like the star!
'Twould be a bargain for a Jew![5]
Say – may I have it – Sir?
—1861

[*I'm Nobody! Who are you?*][6]

I'm Nobody! Who are you?
Are you – Nobody – too?
Then there's a pair of us!
Don't tell! they'd banish us – you know!

5   How dreary – to be – Somebody!
How public – like a Frog –
To tell your name – the livelong June –
To an admiring Bog!
—1861

---

[1]   This poem appears in Johnson as Poem 233; in Franklin as Poem 247; and in Miller as the fourth poem in Sheet 1 of Fascicle 10, page 117. The present text is in complete accord with the transcriptions of Johnson, Franklin, and Miller; the mark at the end of line 3, however, could plausibly be transcribed as a right-slanting comma.

[2]   *Serfs* People in servitude.

[3]   *phosphoric* Phosphorescent, glowing in the dark.

[4]   This poem appears in Johnson as Poem 223; in Franklin as Poem 258; and in Miller as the only poem in Sheet 2 of Fascicle 11, page 127. The present text is in agreement with Franklin and Miller regarding the punctuation of the poem, and with Miller in emending "opon" to "upon" in line 3.

[5]   *'Twould … Jew* I.e., you would get a good deal (Dickinson is referring to the racist stereotype that Jewish people get the better of others in financial dealings).

---

[6]   This poem appears in Johnson as Poem 288; in Franklin as Poem 260; and in Miller as part of Fascicle 11, Sheet 4, page 128. The poem was printed by Todd and Higginson in *Poems* (1891), with "Don't tell" printed at the end of the third line rather than the beginning of the fourth. There is only one manuscript version extant; transcriptions of the fourth line vary. The present editors follow Johnson in emending "Dont" to "Don't," while printing "they'd" in lower case; Franklin transcribes the line as-is ("Dont … they'd"), while Miller emends "Dont" to "Don't" and capitalizes "They'd."

Dickinson provides two variant word choices in the manuscript: "advertise" for "banish" in line 4, and "one's" for "your" in line 7.

A facsimile of the manuscript appears to the right.

+ + 3

I'm Nobody! Who are you?
Are you - Nobody - too?
Then there's a pair of us!
Dont tell! they'd banish
us - you know!   advertise

How dreary - to be - Somebody!
How public - like a Frog -
                 one's
To tell your name - the livelong
June -
To an admiring Bog!

_____

I held a Jewel in my fingers
And went to sleep -
The day was warm, and winds
were prosy -
I said "'Twill keep" -

I woke - and chid my honest
fingers,
The Gem was gone -

X 2

Wild nights - Wild nights!
Were I with thee
Wild nights should be
Our luxury!

Futile - the winds -
to a Heart in port -
Done with the Compass -
Done with the Chart -!

Rowing in Eden -
Ah, the Sea!
Might I but moor -
Tonight -
In thee!

[*Wild nights – Wild nights!*][1]

Wild nights – Wild nights!
Were I with thee
Wild nights should[2] be
Our luxury!

5 Futile – the winds –
To a Heart in port –
Done with the Compass –
Done with the Chart!

Rowing in Eden –
10 Ah – the Sea!
Might I but moor – tonight –
In thee!
—1861

[*Wild nights – Wild nights!*]

Wild nights – Wild nights!
Were I with thee
Wild nights should be
Our luxury!

5 Futile – the winds –
To a Heart in port –
Done with the Compass –
Done with the Chart!

Rowing in Eden –
10 Ah! the Sea!
Might I but moor –
Tonight –
In thee!
—1861

---

[1] This poem appears in Johnson as Poem 249; in Franklin as Poem 269; and in Miller as part of Fascicle 11, Sheet 8, page 133. Here we present first a facsimile of the only manuscript version (see the facing page). Next is a conventional transcription of the poem, according to the principles followed by both Franklin and Miller—with the mark after "Ah" interpreted as a dash, and with "tonight" interpreted as the final word of the eleventh line, written in lower case. The next column presents an alternative transcription, with the mark after "Ah" interpreted as an exclamation mark missing its dot, and "Tonight" read as a capitalized word, forming a line on its own. Given that Dickinson capitalized with great frequency, and that she did not generally indent so as to make it clear if a word at the beginning of a line was intended to be carried over from the previous line or to begin a new line, other readings seem possible as well. Johnson reads the mark after "Ah" as a comma and capitalizes "Tonight," while keeping it as part of the eleventh line.

   Todd and Higginson include the poem in their edition of *Poems*, second series (1891), with "To-night" capitalized and printed at the beginning of the twelfth line rather than at the end of the eleventh; their version is reproduced on the following page.

[2] *should* Would.

[*Wild nights – Wild nights!*]

Wild nights! Wild nights!
Were I with thee,
Wild nights should be
Our luxury!

5   Futile the winds
To a heart in port,
Done with the compass,
Done with the chart.

Rowing in Eden!
10 Ah! the sea!
Might I but moor
To-night in thee!
—1891

[*Over the fence –*][1]

Over the fence –
Strawberries – grow –
Over the fence –
I could climb – if I tried, I know –
5 Berries are nice!

But – if I stained my Apron –
God would certainly scold!
Oh, dear, – I guess if He were a Boy –
He'd – climb – if He could!
—1861

---

1   This poem appears in Johnson as Poem 251; in Franklin as Poem 271; and in Miller as the last poem of Fascicle 11, page 134. The present transcription is in agreement with those of all three; it is worth noting, however, that the marks on either side of "dear" could plausibly be read as single quotation marks rather than commas—and that the following mark could easily be read as a comma rather than a dash.

Emily Dickinson, *Herbarium*, c. 1839–46, Seq. 35. Between the ages of about nine and sixteen, Dickinson created a book of pressed flower specimens labeled with their Latin names. Among the plants included on this page is a flower that came to hold significance for Dickinson, the *Monotropa uniflora* (center right), commonly known as the Indian pipe (a name no longer in use), the ghost plant, and the ghost pipe. When Mabel Loomis Todd sent her a drawing of the ghost plant in 1882, Dickinson wrote a letter back, saying: "That without suspecting it you should send me the preferred flower of life, seems almost supernatural, and the sweet glee that I felt at meeting it, I could confide to none" (L769). The ghost plant also features in the 1879 poem "'Tis whiter than an Indian Pipe—".

[*I taste a liquor never brewed –*][1]

I taste a liquor never brewed –
From tankards scooped in Pearl –
Not all the Frankfort Berries[2]
Yield such an alcohol!

5   Inebriate of air – am I –
And Debauchee of Dew –
Reeling, thro' endless summer days,
From inns of molten Blue –

When "Landlords" turn the drunken Bee
10   Out of the foxglove's door –
When Butterflies – renounce their "drams"[3] –
I shall but drink the more!

Till Seraphs[4] swing their snowy Hats –
And Saints – to windows run –
15   To see the little Tippler
From Manzanilla[5] come!
        —1861

The May-Wine.

I taste a liquor never brewed,
    From tankards scooped in pearl;
Not Frankfort berries yield the sense
    Such a delirious whirl.

Inebriate of air am I,
    And debauchee of dew;—
Reeling through endless summer days,
    From inns of molten blue.

When landlords turn the drunken bee
    Out of the Fox-glove's door,
When butterflies renounce their drams,
    I shall but drink the more;

Till seraphs swing their snowy hats,
    And saints to windows run,
To see the little tippler
    Come staggering toward the sun.

---

[1]   This poem appears in Johnson as Poem 214; in Franklin as Poem 207; and in Miller as the first poem in Sheet 1 of Fascicle 12, page 135 [the 1859 version] and also as the third poem in Sheet 4 of Fascicle 10, pages 122–23 [the 1861 version]. The fascicle manuscripts are the only manuscript versions extant. Dickinson provides two variant readings: "Vats upon the Rhine" for "Frankfort Berries" and "Leaning against the – Sun –" as an alternative last line (Franklin adopts the variant last line in his *Poems of Emily Dickinson*). The present transcription is in agreement with those of Franklin and Miller, except in one particular; we read the small mark at the end of line 7 (which resembles a right-slanting comma) as a comma rather than a dash.
        A variant of this poem (from a now-lost manuscript copy, with a different last line) was published in the *Springfield Republican*, 4 May 1861, under the title "The May-Wine."

[2]   *Frankfort Berries*   Grapes grown in Germany's Rhine Valley.

[3]   *drams*   Small cups of liquor or wine.

[4]   *Seraphs*   Angels.

[5]   *Tippler*   Habitual drinker, but not a full-fledged alcoholic; *Manzanilla*   Spanish sherry.

There's a certain Slant of light,
Winter Afternoons.
That oppresses, like the Heft
Of Cathedral Tunes.

Heavenly Hurt, it gives us.
We can find no scar,
But internal difference
When the Meanings, are.

None may teach it. Any.
'tis the Seal Despair.
An imperial affliction
Sent us of the Air.

When it comes, the Landscape listens.
Shadows. hold their breath.
When it goes, 'tis like the Distance
On the look of Death.

[*There's a certain Slant of light,*][1]

There's a certain Slant of light,
Winter Afternoons –
That oppresses, like the Heft
Of Cathedral Tunes –

5 Heavenly Hurt, it gives us –
We can find no scar,
But internal difference –
Where the Meanings, are –

None may teach it – Any –
10 'Tis the Seal Despair –
An imperial affliction
Sent us of the Air –

When it comes, the Landscape listens –
Shadows – hold their breath –
15 When it goes, 'tis like the Distance
On the look of Death –
—1862

---

[1] This poem appears in Johnson as Poem 258; in Franklin as Poem 320; and in Miller as the fourth poem in Sheet 3, Fascicle 13, page 153. A facsimile of the only manuscript version extant appears to the left (and also, as a larger image, on page 27). Above is a conventional transcription of the poem following the principles established by Johnson, Franklin, and Miller; both Franklin and Miller read the poem as having thirteen dashes. (Johnson reads the mark after "difference" as a comma; in other respects his transcription is identical to those of Franklin and Miller.) The left column on the facing page offers an alternative transcription, with this mark ˌ used to designate punctuation that takes a form resembling a right-slanting comma.

Todd and Higginson edited the poem for their edition of *Poems* (1890), with "weight" replacing "heft" in line 3, and with only one dash; that version is reproduced on the facing page in the right column.

This poem is part of Dickinson's Fascicle 13, which is printed in full on pages 61–67 of this volume.

[*There's a certain Slant of light,*]

There's a certain Slant of light,
Winter Afternoons
That oppresses, like the Heft
Of Cathedral Tunes –

5 Heavenly Hurt, it gives us –
We can find no scar,
But internal difference
Where the Meanings, are –

None may teach it Any –
10 'Tis the Seal Despair –
An imperial affliction
Sent us of the Air –

When it comes, the Landscape listens
Shadows – hold their breath –
15 When it goes, 'tis like the Distance
On the look of Death –
—1862

[*There's a certain Slant of light,*]

There's a certain slant of light,
On winter afternoons,
That oppresses, like the weight
Of cathedral tunes.

5 Heavenly hurt it gives us;
We can find no scar,
But internal difference
Where the meanings are.

None may teach it anything,
10 'Tis the seal, despair, –
An imperial affliction
Sent us of the air.

When it comes, the landscape listens,
Shadows hold their breath;
15 When it goes, 't is like the distance
On the look of death.
—1890

[*"Hope" is the thing with feathers –*][1]

"Hope" is the thing with feathers –
That perches in the soul –
And sings the tune without the words –
And never stops – at all –

5   And sweetest – in the Gale – is heard –
And sore must be the storm –
That could abash the little Bird
That kept so many warm –

I've heard it in the chilliest land
10   And on the strangest Sea –
Yet, never, in Extremity,
It asked a crumb – of Me.
—1862

[*Your Riches – taught me – Poverty.*][2]

Your Riches – taught me – Poverty.
Myself – a Millionaire
In little Wealths, as Girls could boast
Till broad as Buenos Ayre[3] –

5   You drifted your Dominions –
A Different Peru –
And I esteemed All Poverty
For Life's Estate with you –

Of Mines, I little know – myself –
10   But just the names, of Gems –
The Colors of the Commonest –
And scarce of Diadems –

So much, that did I meet the Queen –
Her Glory I should know –
15   But this, must be a different Wealth –
To miss it – beggars so –

I'm sure 'tis India – all Day –
To those who look on You –
Without a stint – without a blame,
20   Might I – but be the Jew[4] –

I'm sure it is Golconda[5] –
Beyond my power to deem –
To have a smile for mine – each Day,
How better, than a Gem!

25   At least, it solaces to know
That there exists – a Gold –
Altho' I prove it, just in time
It's distance – to behold –

It's far – far Treasure to surmise –
30   And estimate the Pearl –
That slipped my simple[6] fingers through –
While just a Girl at school.
—1862

---

[1]   This poem appears in Johnson as Poem 254; in Franklin as Poem 314; and in Miller within Fascicle 13, Sheet 2, page 150. All three of those editors punctuate the poem identically, as have the editors of this anthology—which is an entirely defensible reading, though alternative readings are certainly possible in lines 6, 11, and 12, and perhaps line 4 as well.

[2]   This poem appears in Johnson as Poem 299; in Franklin as Poem 418; and in Miller as the first poem in Sheet 5 of Fascicle 14, pages 165–66. The present text is in agreement with Johnson, Franklin, and Miller regarding the punctuation of the fascicle manuscript of the poem, and with Franklin and Miller in transcribing the "m" in "mine" in line 23 and the "s" in "school" in the poem's final line as lower case rather than capital letters. The marks at the ends of lines 4, 18, 21, and 22 could plausibly be read as right-slanting commas.

   This poem was originally sent as a letter to Dickinson's sister-in-law and dear friend, Susan Gilbert Dickinson. "Dear Sue" was inscribed above the poem, and following it was a simple note: "Dear Sue – You see I remember. Emily." Dickinson also copied the poem into Fascicle 14 and sent a copy to Thomas Wentworth Higginson.

[3]   *Buenos Ayre*   Buenos Aires, here representing the wealth of South America, whose mines of gems and silver had been much discussed in American periodicals during this period; the other place names of this poem, "Peru" and "India," share this association with riches and splendor and were considered sources of exotic luxuries.

[4]   *Jew*   Stereotypes in Dickinson's day often depicted Jewish people as merchants of precious gems.

[5]   *Golconda*   Region in India known for its diamond mines.

[6]   *simple*   Innocent, foolish.

[*I found the words to every thought*][1]

I found the words to every thought
I ever had – but One –
And that – defies me –
As a Hand did try to chalk[2] the Sun

5   To Races – nurtured in the Dark –
How would your own – begin?
Can Blaze be shown in Cochineal[3] –
Or Noon – in Mazarin?[4]
            —1862

[*I like a look of Agony,*][5]

I like a look of Agony,
Because I know it's true –
Men do not sham Convulsion,
Nor simulate, a Throe –

5   The eyes glaze once – and that is Death –
Impossible to feign
The Beads upon the Forehead
By homely Anguish strung.
            —1862

[*I felt a Funeral, in my Brain,*][6]

I felt a Funeral, in my Brain,
And Mourners to and fro
Kept treading – treading – till it seemed
That Sense[7] was breaking through –

5   And when they all were seated,
A Service, like a Drum –
Kept beating – beating – till I thought
My Mind was going numb –

And then I heard them lift a Box
10   And creak across my Soul
With those same Boots of Lead, again,
Then Space – began to toll,

As all the Heavens were a Bell,
And Being, but an Ear,
15   And I, and Silence, some strange Race
Wrecked, solitary, here –

And then a Plank in Reason, broke,
And I dropped down, and down –
And hit a World, at every plunge,
20   And Finished knowing – then –
            —1862

---

[1] This poem appears in Johnson as Poem 581; in Franklin as Poem 436; and in Miller as the last poem in Sheet 5 of Fascicle 15, page 175. Dickinson provides two variant word choices in the fascicle manuscript: "phrase" for "words" in line 1; and "done" for "shown" in line 7.

[2] *chalk*   Sketch, but also "make pale" or whiten.

[3] *Cochineal*   Lustrous scarlet color, made from a dye composed of the desiccated bodies of an insect, the *coccus cacti*, commonly found in Mexico.

[4] *Mazarin*   Deep shade of blue.

[5] This poem appears in Johnson as Poem 339; in Franklin as Poem 241; and in Miller as the second poem in Sheet 2 of Fascicle 16, page 179. All three transcribe the poem in the same way—as is done here.

[6] This poem appears in Johnson as Poem 280; in Franklin as Poem 340; and in Miller as the third poem in Sheet 2 of Fascicle 16, page 179. The present transcription of the fascicle manuscript is in complete agreement with those of Johnson, Franklin, and Miller. There are few transcription issues with the punctuation of the poem; the mark at the end of line 6 could plausibly be read as a right-slanting comma, and the mark at the end of line 8 as a period. Dickinson provides two variant word choices in the manuscript: "Crash" for "plunge" in line 19, and "Got through" for "Finished" in line 20. The poem was first published by Todd and Higginson in *Poems: Third Series* (1896), with the final stanza omitted and numerous smaller changes.

[7] *Sense*   Meaning, but also sensory perception, consciousness.

[*It was not Death, for I stood up,*][1]

It was not Death, for I stood up,
And all the Dead, lie down –
It was not Night, for all the Bells
Put Out their Tongues, for Noon.

5 It was not Frost, for on my Flesh
I felt Siroccos[2] – crawl –
Nor Fire – for just my Marble feet
Could keep a Chancel,[3] cool –

And yet, it tasted, like them all,
10 The Figures I have seen
Set orderly, for Burial,
Reminded me, of mine –

As if my life were shaven,
And fitted to a frame,
15 And could not breathe without a key,
And 'twas like Midnight, some –

When everything that ticked – has stopped –
And Space stares, all around,
Or Grisly frosts – first Autumn morns,
20 Repeal the Beating Ground –

But, most, like Chaos – Stopless – cool –
Without a Chance, or Spar[4] –
Or even a Report of Land –
To justify – Despair.
—1862

---

[1] This poem appears in Johnson as Poem 510; in Franklin as Poem 355; and in Miller as the first poem in Sheet 4 of Fascicle 17, pages 187–88. There is only one manuscript version extant; two alternative readings are written in the margins: "Knees" for "Flesh" in line 5, and "two" for "my" in line 7. Other than in line 18, the transcription here is in accord with the three standard editions. Miller and Johnson both transcribe the punctuation in line 18 as two dashes, while Franklin reads the line as having a dash at the end and no punctuation after "stares." In the manuscript the marks that appear after "stares" and after "around" are similar—both shaped like right-slanting commas.

[2] *Siroccos* Hot, dry winds from North Africa that sweep across the Mediterranean to Southern Europe.

[3] *Chancel* Section of a church where the services are performed.

[4] *Spar* Piece of timber, often used for supportive wooden structures on a ship, such as masts, booms, or gaffs.

[*A Bird came down the Walk –*][5]

A Bird came down the Walk –
He did not know I saw.
He bit an Angleworm[6] in halves
And ate the fellow, raw,

5 And then he drank a Dew
From a convenient Grass –
And then hopped sidewise to the Wall
To let a Beetle pass –

He glanced with rapid eyes
10 That hurried all around –
They looked like frightened Beads, I thought –
He stirred his Velvet Head

Like one in danger, Cautious,
I offered him a Crumb
15 And he unrolled his feathers
And rowed him softer home –

Than Oars divide the Ocean,
Too silver[7] for a seam –
Or Butterflies, off Banks of Noon
20 Leap, plashless as they swim.
—1862

---

[5] This poem appears in Johnson as Poem 328; in Franklin as Poem 359; and in Miller as the third and last poem in Sheet 5 of Fascicle 17, pages 189–90. There are two manuscript versions extant, both evidently from 1862; the punctuation of the two differs in several respects, beginning with the comma that appears after "Bird" in the first line of the version that both Franklin and Miller take as their primary copy text. The present text is (like that in Johnson's edition) transcribed from the variant manuscript; the transcriptions are identical except for the punctuation at the end of the second line, which Johnson reads as a dash. It is one of several points of uncertainty; several of the other dashes could well be read as right-slanting commas.

Another now-lost manuscript version was sent to Higginson, who printed the full poem in his October 1891 *Atlantic Monthly* article on Dickinson (see pages 97–98 of this volume); Todd and Higginson edited the poem for *Poems* (1890), giving it the title "In the Garden."

[6] *Angleworm* Earthworm (like those used by "anglers," or fishers).

[7] *silver* Glistening and in motion, like quicksilver (mercury), as well as silver in color. Dickinson describes the ocean in similar terms elsewhere, for example as an "everywhere of silver."

[*I know that He exists.*]¹

I know that He exists.
Somewhere – in Silence –
He has hid his rare life
From our gross eyes.

5 'Tis an instant's play.
'Tis a fond Ambush –
Just to make Bliss
Earn her own surprise!

But – should the play
10 Prove piercing earnest –
Should the glee – glaze –
In Death's – stiff – stare –

Would not the fun
Look too expensive!
15 Would not the jest –
Have crawled too far!
—1862

[*After great pain, a formal feeling comes –*]²

After great pain, a formal feeling comes –
The Nerves sit ceremonious, like Tombs –
The stiff Heart questions 'was it He, that bore,'
And 'Yesterday, or Centuries before'?

5 The Feet, mechanical, go round –
A Wooden way
Of Ground, or Air, or Ought –
Regardless grown,
A Quartz contentment, like a stone –

10 This is the Hour of Lead –
Remembered, if outlived,
As Freezing persons, recollect the Snow –
First – Chill – then Stupor – then the letting go –
—1862

[*This World is not conclusion.*]³

This World is not conclusion.
A Species⁴ stands beyond –
Invisible, as Music –
But positive, as Sound –
5 It beckons, and it baffles –
Philosophy, don't know –
And through a Riddle, at the last –
Sagacity, must go –
To guess it, puzzles scholars –
10 To gain it, Men have borne
Contempt of Generations
And Crucifixion, shown –
Faith slips – and laughs, and rallies –
Blushes, if any see –
15 Plucks at a twig of Evidence –
And asks a Vane,⁵ the way –

---

1 This poem appears in Johnson as Poem 338; in Franklin as Poem 365; and in Miller as the first poem in Sheet 2 of Fascicle 18, pages 193–94. There is one manuscript version extant, with little disagreement over the transcription. The present text agrees with Johnson in transcribing the mark at the end of line 5 as a period; both Franklin and Miller transcribe it as a dash.

2 This poem appears in Johnson as Poem 341; in Franklin as Poem 372; and in Miller as the third poem in Sheet 4 of Fascicle 18, page 198. The manuscript transcriptions by Franklin and Miller diverge in several respects from that by Johnson—most notably in that Johnson does not transcribe the quotation marks, and ignores the manuscript marks regarding the ordering of the lines in the second stanza. The present text agrees with those of Franklin and of Miller in every particular; it may be worth noting, however, that the mark at the end of line 7 could perhaps more plausibly be read as a right-slanting comma than as a dash, and that the mark after "First" in the last line appears to be a dot rather than a dash.

---

3 This poem appears in Johnson as Poem 501; in Franklin as Poem 373; and in Miller as the fourth poem in Sheet 4 of Fascicle 18, pages 198–99. There are several alternatives indicated in the manuscript: "sequel" for "Species" in line 2; "prove" for "guess" in line 9; "Sure" for "Strong" in line 18; and "Mouse" for "Tooth" in line 19. The transcriptions by Johnson, Franklin, and Miller are in agreement except in one particular; Franklin does not emend "dont" to "don't" in line 6. The present text agrees with those of Franklin and of Miller; it is worth noting, however, that several of the marks at the ends of lines could plausibly be read as right-slanting commas, and at least two others as periods.

4 *Species* Metaphysical ideal or vision.

5 *Vane* Weather vane.

Much Gesture, from the Pulpit –
Strong Hallelujahs roll –
Narcotics cannot still the – Tooth
20   That nibbles at the soul –
—1862

[*I like to see it lap the Miles –*][1]

I like to see it lap the Miles –
And lick the Valleys up –
And stop to feed itself at Tanks[2] –
And then – prodigious step

5   Around a Pile of Mountains –
And supercilious peer
In Shanties – by the sides of Roads –
And then a Quarry pare

To fit its sides
10   And crawl between
Complaining all the while
In horrid – hooting stanza –
Then chase itself down Hill –

And neigh like Boanerges[3] –
15   Then – prompter than a Star
Stop – docile and omnipotent
At its own stable door –
—1862

[*The Soul selects her own Society –*][4]

The Soul selects her own Society –
Then – shuts the Door –
To her divine Majority –
Present no more –

5   Unmoved – she notes the Chariots – pausing –
At her low Gate –
Unmoved – an Emperor be kneeling
Upon her Mat

I've known her – from an ample nation –
10   Choose One –
Then – close the Valves of her attention –
Like Stone –
—1862

[*One need not be a Chamber – to be Haunted –*][5]

One need not be a Chamber – to be Haunted –
One need not be a House –

---

[1]   This poem appears in Johnson as Poem 585; in Franklin as Poem 383; and in Miller as the second poem in Sheet 2 of Fascicle 19, page 204. Franklin leaves "it's" uncorrected both in line 9 and in line 17; Dickinson provides several alternative readings in the fascicle manuscript: "hear it" for "see it" in line 1; "Ribs" for "sides" in line 9; "then" for "And" in line 14; and "punctual" for "prompter" in line 15. Todd and Higginson edited the poem for *Poems* (1890), giving it the title "The Railway Train."

[2]   *Tanks* Water stations (also called "water stops") for steam engines, where they could replenish their supply of water.

[3]   *Boanerges* Loud, denunciatory preacher.

[4]   This poem appears in Johnson as Poem 303; in Franklin as Poem 409; and in Miller as the last poem in Sheet 4 of Fascicle 20, page 218. The present transcription of the fascicle manuscript is in complete agreement with those of the three standard editions; it is worth noting, however, that several of the marks at the ends of lines (notably, at the ends of lines 1, 3, 5, and 11) could plausibly be read as a right-slanting commas—as could the marks after "Chariots" in line 5 and "her" in line 9. Todd and Higginson include the poem under the title "Exclusion" in *Poems* (1890); they adopt the variant word choices Dickinson provides for lines 3 and 4: "On" for "To" in line 3, and "Obtrude" for "Present" in line 4. Dickinson also provides manuscript variant readings for line 8 ("On her Rush mat") and line 11 ("lids" for "Valves").

[5]   This poem appears in Johnson as Poem 670; in Franklin as Poem 407; and in Miller as the first poem in Sheet 4 of Fascicle 20, page 217. The present editors follow Johnson and Franklin in transcribing from the 1864 variant that Dickinson sent to Susan Dickinson; it differs in several small particulars from the 1862 fascicle text, and in one large one: the fascicle text ends with "More near" rather than "Or More." The fascicle manuscript also includes numerous variants. Like Johnson (but unlike Franklin), we emend "it's" to "its" in line 7. Todd and Higginson include the poem in *Poems* (1891) under the title "Ghosts," evidently using the fascicle manuscript as their base text, but adopting Dickinson's variant word choice for line 8 ("Whiter" for "cooler").

Train engine, 1865 (Library of Congress).

Section of the Atlantic and Great Western Railway, 1862 (National Gallery of Art). In the early 1860s American trains typically traveled at a speed of 30–40 miles per hour.

The Brain has Corridors – surpassing
Material Place –

5   Far safer, of a Midnight Meeting
External Ghost
Than its interior Confronting –
That Cooler Host.

Far safer, through an Abbey gallop,[1]
10   The Stones a'chase –
Than Unarmed, one's a'self encounter –
In lonesome Place –

Ourself behind ourself, concealed –
Should startle most –
15   Assassin hid in our Apartment
Be Horror's least.

The Body – borrows a Revolver –
He bolts the Door –
O'erlooking a superior spectre –
20   Or More –
—1862, 1864

[*They shut me up in Prose –*][2]

They shut me up in Prose –
As when a little Girl
They put me in the Closet –
Because they liked me "still" –

5   Still! Could themself have peeped –
And seen my Brain – go round –

They might as wise have lodged a Bird
For Treason – in the Pound –

Himself[3] has but to will
10   And easy as a Star
Look down upon Captivity –
And laugh – No more have I –
—1862

[*This was a Poet –*][4]

This was a Poet –
It is That
Distills amazing sense
From ordinary Meanings –
5   And Attar[5] so immense

From the familiar species
That perished by the Door –
We wonder it was not Ourselves
Arrested[6] it – before –

10   Of Pictures, the Discloser –
The Poet – it is He –
Entitles Us – by Contrast –
To ceaseless Poverty –

Of Portion – so unconscious –
15   The Robbing – could not harm –
Himself – to Him – a Fortune –
Exterior – to Time –
—1862

---

1   *through an Abbey gallop* Abbeys—usually haunted—are common settings in Gothic literature.

2   This poem appears in Johnson as Poem 613; in Franklin as Poem 445; and in Miller as the last poem in Sheet 2 of Fascicle 21, page 223. The present transcription of the fascicle manuscript is in complete agreement with those of Johnson and Miller; Franklin prints "opon" (for "upon") in line 11, rather than silently correcting, as is done by other editors. It is worth noting that several of the marks at the ends of lines (notably, at the ends of lines 1, 3, 5, 6, and 11) could plausibly be read as right-slanting commas. The manuscript provides a variant of line 11: "Abolish his Captivity" for "Look down upon Captivity."

3   *Himself* I.e., the bird.

4   This poem appears in Johnson as Poem 448; in Franklin as Poem 446; and in Miller as the first poem in Sheet 3 of Fascicle 21, page 224. The present transcription of the fascicle manuscript is in complete agreement with those of Franklin and Miller; Johnson reads what appear in the manuscript to be the poem's first two lines as one, thus regularizing the poem into stanzas of four lines each. It is worth noting that several of the marks at the ends of lines (notably, at the ends of lines 1, 4, 10, and 12) could plausibly be read as right-slanting commas.

5   *Attar* Essential oil made from roses.

6   *Arrested* Caught, laid hold of.

[*I died for Beauty – but was scarce*]¹

I died for Beauty – but was scarce
Adjusted in the Tomb
When One who died for Truth, was lain
In an adjoining Room

5   He questioned softly "Why I failed"?
"For Beauty", I replied –
"And I – for Truth – Themself are One –
We Brethren, are", He said –

And so, as Kinsmen, met a Night –
10   We talked between the Rooms –
Until the Moss had reached our lips –
And covered up – our names –
—1862

[*The Malay – took the Pearl –*]²

The Malay³ – took the Pearl –
Not – I – the Earl –
I – feared the Sea – too much
Unsanctified – to touch –

5   Praying that I might be
Worthy – the Destiny –
The Swarthy fellow swam –
And bore my Jewel – Home –

Home to the Hut! What lot
10   Had I – the Jewel – got –
Borne on a Dusky Breast –
I had not deemed a Vest
Of Amber – fit –

The Negro⁴ never knew
15   I – wooed it – too
To gain, or be undone –
Alike to Him – One –
—1862

---

1   This poem appears in Johnson as Poem 449; in Franklin as Poem 448; and in Miller as the third poem in Sheet 3 of Fascicle 21, page 225. The present transcription of the fascicle manuscript is in complete agreement with that of Johnson, who emends "bretheren" to "brethren." (Franklin and Miller print the word with the additional "e.") The word was spelled (and presumably pronounced) with three syllables in late medieval times ("bretheryn"), though by Shakespeare's time it had become standardized as a two-syllable word. It is certainly possible that Dickinson intended the archaic spelling and pronunciation, but it seems at least as likely that this was an inadvertent misspelling; Dickinson was, as Miller says, "an erratic speller." It is also worth noting that, with the two-syllable "brethren," the line scans as iambic trimeter—as do the last lines of the other two stanzas.

There are few transcription issues with the punctuation of the poem, though the marks at the ends of lines 10 and 11 could plausibly be read as right-slanting commas.

---

2   This poem appears in Johnson as Poem 452; in Franklin as Poem 451; and in Miller as the third poem in Sheet 4 of Fascicle 21, page 226. The present text is in agreement with Johnson, Franklin, and Miller regarding the punctuation of the poem—though the mark at the end of line 7 could plausibly be read as a right-slanting comma.

3   *Malay* Person from the Malay Peninsula. Prior to the industrialization of the pearl industry, many pearls were harvested by divers in Southeast Asia.

4   *Negro* In the nineteenth century, this term was often used to refer to any person perceived as having dark skin.

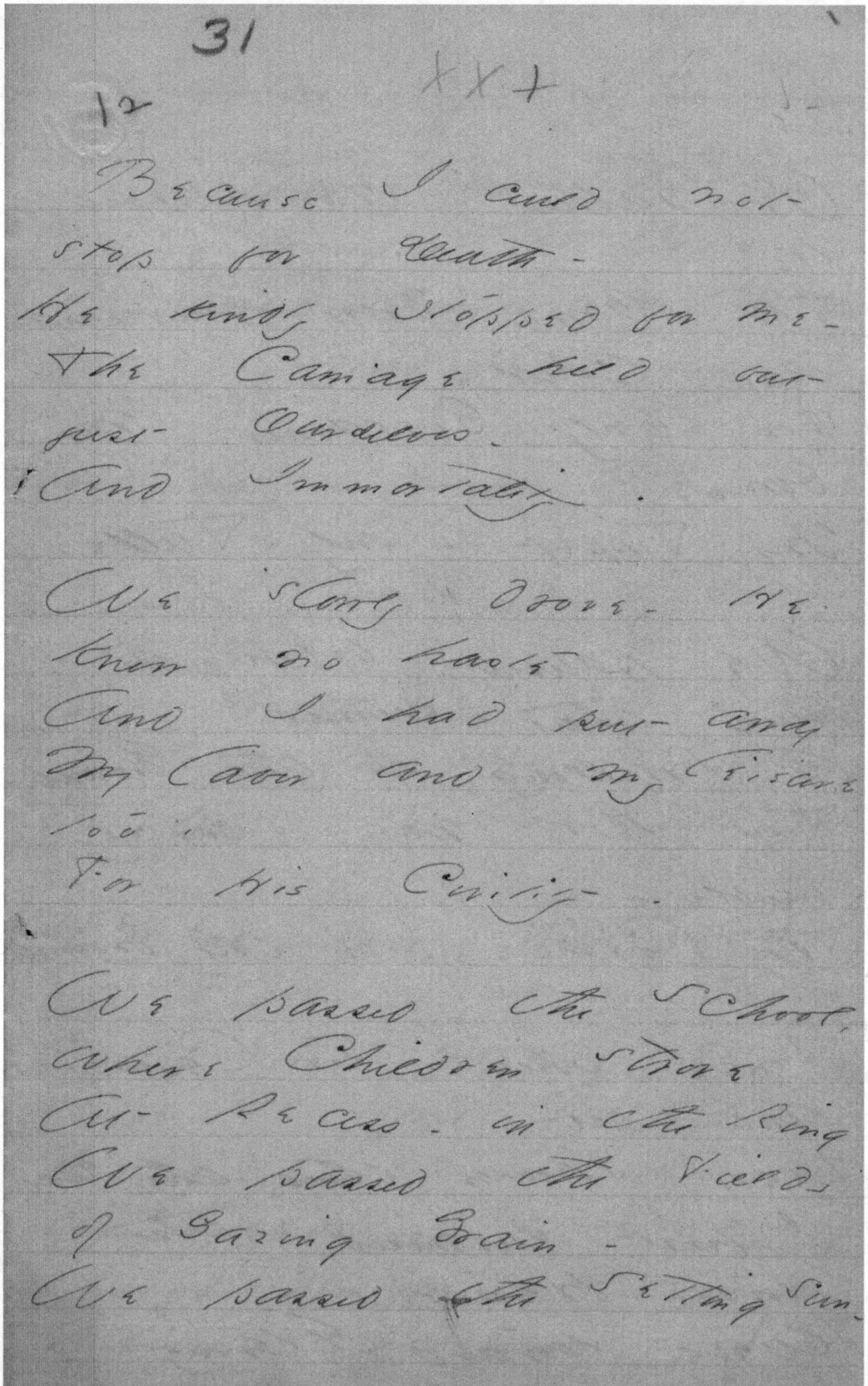
31

12

Because I could not
stop for Death -
He kindly stopped for me -
The Carriage held but -
just - Ourselves.
And Immortality.

We slowly drove - He
knew no haste
And I had put away
My Labor and my Leisure
too,
For His Civility -

We passed the School,
where Children strove
At Recess - in the Ring
We passed the Fields
of Gazing Grain -
We passed the Setting Sun.

Or rather - He passed
Us -
The Dews drew quivering
and Chill -
For only Gossamer, my
Gown -
My Tippet - only Tulle -

We paused before a
House that seemed
A Swelling of the Ground -
The Roof was scarcely
visible -
The Cornice - in the Ground -

Since then - 'tis Centuries
and yet
Feels shorter than the Day
I first surmised the
Horses' Heads
Were toward Eternity -

[*Because I could not stop for Death* –][1]

Because I could not stop for Death –
He kindly stopped for me –
The Carriage held but just Ourselves –
And Immortality.

5 We slowly drove – He knew no haste
And I had put away
My labor and my leisure too,
For His Civility –

We passed the School, where Children strove[2]
10 At Recess – in the Ring –
We passed the Fields of Gazing Grain –
We passed the Setting Sun –

Or rather – He passed Us –
The Dews drew quivering and Chill –
15 For only Gossamer,[3] my Gown –
My Tippet – only Tulle[4] –

We paused before a House that seemed
A Swelling of the Ground –
The Roof was scarcely visible –
20 The Cornice[5] – in the Ground –

Since then – 'tis Centuries – and yet
Feels shorter than the Day
I first surmised the Horses' Heads
Were toward Eternity –
—1862

[*Our journey had advanced* –][6]

Our journey had advanced –
Our feet were almost come
To that odd Fork in Being's Road –
Eternity – by Term

5 Our pace took sudden awe –
Our feet – reluctant – led –
Before – were Cities – but Between –
The Forest of the Dead –

Retreat – was Out of Hope –
10 Behind – a Sealed Route –
Eternity's White Flag – Before –
And God – at every Gate –
—1862

---

[1] This poem appears in Johnson as Poem 712; in Franklin as Poem 479; and in Miller as the opening poem in Fascicle 23, Sheet 1, page 239. The fascicle version (reproduced on the preceding pages) is the only manuscript version extant. The transcriptions in the Johnson, Franklin, and Miller editions are in complete accord, interpreting the marks at the ends of lines 3, 12, 13, and 24 as dashes, and the mark after "Centuries" in line 21 as a dash as well; the transcription here takes the same approach. Alternative transcriptions are certainly conceivable, however, given that many of the marks which have traditionally been read as dashes take a form more suggestive of right-slanting commas.

    The Todd and Higginson edition of *Poems* (1890) includes a version of this poem, under the title "The Chariot," in which there are several substantive changes—including the omission of the fourth stanza.

[2] *strove* Fought or quarreled.

[3] *Gossamer* Extremely fine material.

[4] *Tippet* Small shawl or capelet; *Tulle* Fine, netted fabric.

[5] *Cornice* Decorative molding that runs along the base of a building's roof.

[6] This poem appears in Johnson as Poem 615; in Franklin as Poem 453; and in Miller as the first poem in Sheet 5 of Fascicle 21, page 227. The present text is in full accord with the transcriptions of Johnson, Franklin, and Miller—though it may be noted that the mark at the end of line 7 could plausibly be read as a right-slanting comma. The poem was first published by Todd and Higginson in *Poems* (1891), under the title "The Journey."

[*I dwell in Possibility –*][1]

I dwell in Possibility –
A fairer House than Prose –
More numerous of Windows –
Superior – for Doors –

5 Of Chambers as the Cedars –
Impregnable of Eye –
And for an Everlasting Roof
The Gambrels[2] of the Sky –

Of Visitors – the fairest –
10 For Occupation – This
The spreading wide my narrow Hands
To gather Paradise –
—1862

[*He fumbles at your Soul*][3]

He fumbles at your Soul
As Players at the Keys[4]
Before they drop full Music on –
He stuns you by degrees –
5 Prepares your brittle nature
For the ethereal Blow
By fainter Hammers – further heard –
Then nearer – Then so slow
Your Breath has time to straighten –
10 Your Brain – to bubble Cool –
Deals – One – imperial – Thunderbolt –
That scalps your naked Soul –

When Winds take Forests in their Paws –
The Universe – is still –
—1862

[*It feels a shame to be Alive –*][5]

It feels a shame to be Alive –
When Men so brave – are dead –
One envies the Distinguished Dust –
Permitted – such a Head –

---

[3] This poem appears in Johnson as Poem 315; in Franklin as Poem 477; and in Miller as the third poem in Sheet 6 of Fascicle 22, pages 237–38. Miller transcribes from the fascicle manuscript, in which "substance" appears instead of "nature" in line 5; "chance" instead of "time" in line 9; "peels" instead of "scalps" in line 12; and "Firmaments – are" instead of "Universe – is" in line 14. The variant readings are included in the fascicle manuscript, and were adopted in the manuscript version sent to Susan Dickinson (also believed to date from late 1862), which is the basis for the present text. The first 12 lines in the fascicle version are organized into three four-line stanzas. Franklin's Poem 477 adopts all the variant readings of the Susan Dickinson version, but adopts the stanza structure of the fascicle version. Both Franklin and Miller retain the misspelling of "ethereal" as "etherial," which appears in both versions. There are few transcription issues with the punctuation of this poem.

[4] *Keys* I.e., piano keys.

[5] This poem appears in Johnson as Poem 444; in Franklin as Poem 524; and in Miller as the second poem in Sheet 6 of Fascicle 24, pages 257–58. The present text is in agreement with the transcriptions of both Franklin and Miller. It is perhaps worth noting that nineteenth-century reading habits in a poetic context such as line 15 of this poem would almost certainly have taken "dissolved" as having three syllables (dis-sol-ved).

---

[1] This poem appears in Johnson as Poem 657; in Franklin as Poem 466; and in Miller as the first poem in Sheet 4 of Fascicle 22, page 233. The present transcription of the fascicle manuscript is in complete agreement with those of all three of these editors—all of whom silently emend "visiters" in line 9. There are few transcription issues with the punctuation of the poem, though the mark at the end of line 5 could plausibly be read as a right-slanting comma. Dickinson provides one alternative reading in the manuscript—"Gables" for "Gambrels" in line 8.

[2] *Gambrels* Roofs with two slopes on each side. (This variety of roof was common in the northeastern states.)

5 The Stone – that tells defending Whom
   This Spartan put away[1]
   What little of Him we – possessed
   In Pawn for Liberty

   The price is great – Sublimely paid –
10 Do we deserve – a Thing –
   That lives – like Dollars – must be piled
   Before we may obtain?

   Are we that wait – sufficient worth –
   That such Enormous Pearl
15 As life – dissolved be[2] – for Us –
   In Battle's – horrid Bowl?

   It may be – a Renown to live –
   I think the Men who die –
   Those unsustained – Saviors –
20 Present Divinity –
   —1863

[*This is my letter to the World*][3]

   This is my letter to the World
   That never wrote to Me –
   The simple News that Nature told –
   With tender Majesty

5 Her Message is committed
   To Hands I cannot see –
   For love of Her – Sweet – countrymen –
   Judge tenderly – of Me
   —1863

[*I'm sorry for the Dead – Today –*][4]

   I'm sorry for the Dead – Today –
   It's such congenial times
   Old Neighbors have at fences –
   It's time o' year for Hay.

5 And Broad – Sunburned Acquaintance
   Discourse between the Toil –
   And laugh, a homely species
   That makes the Fences smile –

   It seems so straight to lie away
10 From all the noise of Fields –
   The Busy Carts – the fragrant Cocks[5] –
   The Mower's Metre[6] – Steals

   A Trouble lest they're homesick –
   Those Farmers – and their Wives –
15 Set separate from the Farming –
   And all the Neighbor's lives –

   A Wonder if the Sepulchre
   Don't feel a lonesome way –
   When Men – and Boys – and Carts – and June,
20 Go down the Fields to "Hay" –
   —1863

---

1 *The Stone ... put away* Allusion to the famous epitaph at the site of the Battle of Thermopylae (480 BCE), where all 300 of the Spartan soldiers who were sent to defend Greece against the Persian army died; one translation of the epitaph reads, "Go tell the Spartans, thou who passest by, / That here, obedient to their laws, we lie."

2 *Enormous Pearl ... dissolved be* Reference to the commonly held belief that pearls dissolve in strongly acidic solutions. See also Matthew 13.45–46: "Again, the kingdom of heaven is like unto a merchant man, seeking goodly pearls; Who, when he had found one pearl of great price, went and sold all that he had, and bought it."

3 This poem appears in Johnson as Poem 441; in Franklin as Poem 519; and in Miller as the second poem in Sheet 4 of Fascicle 24, page 254. The present transcription of the fascicle manuscript is in complete agreement with those of all three of these editors. There are few transcription issues with the punctuation of the poem, though the marks at the ends of lines 2 and 6 could plausibly be read as periods rather than dashes.

4 This poem appears in Johnson as Poem 529; in Franklin as Poem 582; and in Miller as the first poem in Sheet 5 of Fascicle 25, page 266. Franklin leaves "Dont" uncorrected in line 18, whereas Miller emends to "Don't"; in other respects the present text is in agreement with the transcriptions of both Franklin and Miller. It is worth noting, however, that many of the dashes in the last two stanzas of the poem could plausibly be read as right-slanting commas.

5 *Cocks* I.e., haycocks, or piles of hay.

6 *The Mower's Metre* I.e., the rhythm of the scythe.

[*I heard a Fly buzz – when I died –*][1]

I heard a Fly buzz – when I died –
The Stillness in the Room
Was like the Stillness in the Air –
Between the Heaves of Storm –

5 The Eyes around – had wrung them dry –
And Breaths were gathering firm
For that last Onset – when the King
Be witnessed – in the Room –

I willed my Keepsakes – Signed away
10 What portion of me be
Assignable – and then it was
There interposed a Fly –

With Blue – uncertain stumbling Buzz –
Between the light – and me –
15 And then the Windows failed – and then
I could not see to see
—1863

[*The Brain – is wider than the Sky –*][2]

The Brain – is wider than the Sky –
For – put them side by side –
The one the other will contain
With ease – and You – beside –

5 The Brain is deeper than the sea –
For – hold them – Blue to Blue –
The one the other will absorb –
As Sponges – Buckets – do –

The Brain is just the weight of God –
10 For – Heft them – Pound for Pound –
And they will differ – if they do –
As Syllable from Sound –
—1863

[*There's been a Death, in the Opposite House,*][3]

There's been a Death, in the Opposite House,
As lately as Today –
I know it, by the numb look
Such Houses have – alway[4] –

5 The Neighbors rustle in and Out –
The Doctor – drives away –
A Window opens like a Pod –
Abrupt – mechanically –

Somebody flings a Mattress Out –
10 The Children hurry by –
They wonder if it died – on that –
I used to – when a Boy

The Minister – goes stiffly in –
As if the House were His –
15 And He owned all the Mourners – now –
And little Boys – besides –

---

[1] This poem appears in Johnson as Poem 465; in Franklin as Poem 591; and in Miller as the third poem in Sheet 1 of Fascicle 26, page 270. The present transcription of the fascicle manuscript is in complete agreement with those of Franklin and Miller. There are few transcription issues with the punctuation of the poem, though the marks at the ends of lines 3 and 12 could plausibly be read as right-slanting commas. The second dash in line 13—if dash it is—takes the form of an underline mark beneath the "s" of "stumbling"; Johnson does not read there as being any punctuation mark here.

[2] This poem appears in Johnson as Poem 632; in Franklin as Poem 598; and in Miller as the third poem in Sheet 3 of Fascicle 26, page 273. The present transcription of the fascicle manuscript is in complete agreement with those of Johnson, Franklin, and Miller. There are few transcription issues with the punctuation of the poem; the mark at the end of line 11 could plausibly be read as a right-slanting comma, and the mark at the end of line 12 as a period. Dickinson provides one variant word choice in the manuscript: "include" for "contain" in line 3.

[3] This poem appears in Johnson as Poem 389; in Franklin as Poem 547; and in Miller as the first poem in Sheet 1 of Fascicle 27, page 279. The present transcription of the fascicle manuscript is in complete agreement with those of Johnson, Franklin, and Miller, except in one particular; Franklin spells "mattrass" just as the word appears in Dickinson's manuscript, whereas other editors correct the spelling error. There are few transcription issues with the punctuation of the poem; the marks at the end of lines 11, 20, and 23 could plausibly be read as right-slanting commas, as could the mark after "Milliner" in line 17. Dickinson does not provide any variant words in the manuscript.

[4] *alway* Always.

And then the Milliner[1] – and the Man
Of the Appalling Trade[2] –
To take the measure of the House –
20 There'll be that Dark Parade –

Of Tassels – and of Coaches – soon –
It's easy as a Sign –
The Intuition of the News –
In just a Country Town –
—1863

[*I measure every Grief I meet*][3]

I measure every Grief I meet
With narrow, probing, Eyes –
I wonder if It weighs like Mine –
Or has an Easier size.

5   I wonder if They bore it long –
Or did it just begin –
I could not tell the Date of Mine –
It feels so old a pain –

I wonder if it hurts to live –
10 And if They have to try –
And whether – could They choose between –
It would not be – to die –

I note that Some – gone patient long –
At length, renew their smile –

15 An imitation of a Light
That has so little Oil[4] –

I wonder if when Years have piled –
Some Thousands – on the Harm –
That hurt them early – such a lapse
20 Could give them any Balm[5] –

Or would they go on aching still
Through Centuries of Nerve –
Enlightened to a larger Pain –
In Contrast with the Love –

25 The Grieved – are many – I am told –
There is the various Cause –
Death – is but one – and comes but once –
And only nails the eyes –

There's Grief of Want – and Grief of Cold –
30 A sort they call "Despair" –
There's Banishment from native Eyes –
In sight of Native Air –

And though I may not guess the kind –
Correctly – yet to me
35 A piercing Comfort it affords
In passing Calvary[6] –

To note the fashions – of the Cross –
And how they're mostly worn –
Still fascinated to presume
40 That Some – are like My Own –
—1863

---

[1] *Milliner* Maker of hats and other clothing accessories (in this context, to measure for mourning garments).

[2] *the Man ... Appalling Trade* I.e., the undertaker.

[3] This poem appears in Johnson as Poem 561; in Franklin as Poem 550; and in Miller as the first poem in Sheet 2 of Fascicle 27, pages 280–81. There are few transcription issues with the punctuation of the poem, though there are several with its capitalization. Franklin reads "eyes" in line 2, while both Franklin and Miller read "my own" in the poem's final line; in all those cases the present reading agrees with that of Johnson. Johnson, however, includes a dash between "my" and "own" in the final line, a point at which no punctuation is apparent in the manuscript. Dickinson provides one variant phrase: "With analytic eyes" in line 2.

---

[4] *so little Oil* Reference to an oil lamp in which the fuel is running low.

[5] *Balm* Soothing ointment.

[6] *Calvary* Site where Jesus was crucified.

[*Much Madness is divinest Sense –*][1]

Much Madness is divinest Sense –
To a discerning Eye –
Much Sense – the starkest Madness –
'Tis the Majority
5 In this, as all, prevail –
Assent – and you are sane –
Demur – you're straightway dangerous –
And handled with a Chain –
—1863

[*I started Early – Took my Dog –*][2]

I started Early – Took my Dog –
And visited the Sea –
The Mermaids in the Basement
Came out to look at me –

5 And Frigates – in the Upper Floor
Extended Hempen[3] Hands –
Presuming Me to be a Mouse –
Aground – upon the Sands –

But no Man moved Me – till the Tide
10 Went past my simple Shoe –

And past my Apron – and my Belt
And past my Boddice – too –

And made as He would eat me up –
As wholly as a Dew
15 Upon a Dandelion's Sleeve –
And then – I started – too –

And He – He followed – close behind –
I felt His Silver Heel
Upon my Ankle – Then my Shoes
20 Would overflow with Pearl –

Until We met the Solid Town –
No One He seemed to know –
And bowing – with a Mighty look –
At me – The Sea withdrew –
—1863

[*That I did always love*][4]

That I did always love
I bring thee Proof
That till I loved
I never lived – Enough –

5 That I shall love alway[5] –
I argue thee
That love is life –
And life hath Immortality –

This – dost thou doubt – Sweet –
10 Then have I
Nothing to show
But Calvary[6]
—1863

---

[1] This poem appears in Johnson as Poem 435; in Franklin as Poem 620; and in Miller as the fourth poem in Sheet 3 of Fascicle 29, page 304. Johnson and Franklin read "All" rather than "all" in line 5; a comparison of Dickinson's rendering in line 6 of a capital "A" followed by lower case letters (in "Assent") lends support to Miller's reading of the "a" in "all" as lower case.

[2] This poem appears in Johnson as Poem 520; in Franklin as Poem 656; and in Miller as the first poem in Sheet 2 of Fascicle 30, pages 311–12. The present text follows Johnson in emending all three of the obvious misspellings in the manuscript: "opon" in line 8, and again in line 19; and "Ancle" in line 19. Franklin leaves all three uncorrected, while Miller emends "opon" but not "Ancle." The present text is in agreement with Johnson, Franklin, and Miller regarding the punctuation of the poem. The mark in the middle of line 11 could plausibly be read as a right-slanting comma, and the mark at the end of line 4 could plausibly be read as a period.

[3] *Hempen* Hemp fiber was and is commonly used to make ropes; in the nineteenth century it was also (somewhat less commonly) used to make ships' sails.

[4] This poem appears in Johnson as Poem 549; in Franklin as Poem 652; and in Miller as the last poem in Sheet 6 of Fascicle 31, page 329. The present text is in complete agreement with the transcriptions of Johnson, Franklin, and Miller. Dickinson provides three variant phrases in the fascicle manuscript: "did not live" for "never lived" in line 4; "offer" for "argue" in line 6; and "be" for "is" in line 7.

[5] *alway* Always.

[6] *Calvary* Site of Jesus' crucifixion.

[*What Soft – Cherubic Creatures –*][1]

What Soft – Cherubic Creatures –
These Gentlewomen are –
One would as soon assault a Plush –
Or violate a Star –

5 Such Dimity[2] Convictions –
A Horror so refined
Of freckled Human Nature –
Of Deity – Ashamed –

It's such a common – Glory –
10 A Fisherman's – Degree –
Redemption – Brittle Lady –
Be so – ashamed of Thee.
—1863

[*My Life had stood – a Loaded Gun –*][3]

My Life had stood – a Loaded Gun –
In Corners – till a Day
The Owner passed – identified –
And carried Me away –

5 And now We roam in Sovreign Woods –
And now We hunt the Doe –
And every time I speak for Him –
The Mountains straight reply –

And do I smile, such cordial light
10 Upon the Valley glow –
It is as a Vesuvian[4] face
Had let its pleasure through –

And when at Night – Our good Day done –
I guard My Master's Head –
15 'Tis better than the Eider-Duck's[5]
Deep Pillow – to have shared –

To foe of His – I'm deadly foe –
None stir the second time –
On whom I lay a Yellow Eye –
20 Or an emphatic Thumb –

Though I than He – may longer live
He longer must – than I –
For I have but the power to kill,
Without – the power to die –
—1863

---

[1]   This poem appears in Johnson as Poem 401; in Franklin as Poem 675; and in Miller as the third poem in Sheet 1 of "Unbound Sheets," page 418. Johnson and Miller read "Ashamed" as lower case both in line 8 and in line 12; Franklin reads the word as capitalized in line 8 but lowercase in line 12. Johnson, Franklin, and Miller all read a dash rather than a period at the end of the poem.

[2]   *Dimity*   Lightweight cotton.

[3]   This poem appears in Johnson as Poem 754; in Franklin as Poem 764; and in Miller as the first poem in Sheet 4 of Fascicle 34, pages 354–55. The present transcription of the fascicle manuscript is with two exceptions in agreement with those of Johnson, Franklin, and Miller: Franklin spells "it's" in line 12 just as the word appears in Dickinson's manuscript, whereas other editors correct the error; Franklin and Miller both omit the mark that appears between "Eider" and "Duck" in line 15, whereas (like Johnson) the present editors transcribe it as a hyphen. There are a few other possible transcription issues with the punctuation of the poem; the marks at the end of lines 14 and 19 could plausibly be read as right-slanting commas, while the mark at the end of line 22 could very plausibly be read as a period. Dickinson provides four alternative readings in the manuscript: "the" for "in" in line 5; "Low" for "Deep" in line 16; "harm" for "stir" in line 18; and "art" for "power" in line 23.

[4]   *Vesuvian*   The southern Italian volcano Mount Vesuvius erupted in 79 CE, killing well over one thousand people, primarily in the city of Pompeii.

[5]   *Eider-Duck*   Genus of sea ducks, whose feathers are commonly used to stuff quilts and pillows.

[*"Nature" is what We see –*][1]

"Nature" is what We see –
The Hill – the Afternoon –
Squirrel – Eclipse – the Bumble bee –
Nay – Nature is Heaven –

5 Nature is what We hear –
The Bobolink[2] – the Sea –
Thunder – the Cricket –
Nay – Nature is Harmony –

"Nature" is what We know –
10 Yet have no art to say –
So impotent Our Wisdom is
To Her Sincerity –
—1863

[*I could bring You Jewels – had I a mind to –*][3]

I could bring You Jewels – had I a mind to –
But You have enough – of those –
I could bring You Odors from St Domingo[4] –

Colors – from Vera Cruz[5] –

5 Berries[6] of the Bahamas – have I –
But this little Blaze
Flickering to itself – in the Meadow –
Suits Me – more than those –

Never a Fellow matched this Topaz –
10 And his Emerald Swing –
Dower[7] itself – for Bobadilo[8] –
Better – Could I bring?
—1863

[*Publication – is the Auction*][9]

Publication – is the Auction
Of the Mind of Man –
Poverty – be justifying
For so foul a thing

5 Possibly – but We – would rather
From Our Garret go
White – Unto the White Creator –
Than invest – Our Snow –

Thought belong to Him who gave it –
10 Then – to Him Who bear
It's Corporeal illustration – Sell
The Royal Air –

1 This poem appears in Johnson as Poem 668; in Franklin as Poem 721; and in Miller as the third poem in Sheet 2 of Fascicle 35, page 361. Johnson transcribes from a variant that Dickinson sent to Susan Dickinson; it differs in several small particulars and two large ones: the poem is not divided into stanzas, and "Simplicity" is substituted for "Sincerity" in the final line. The present text follows Franklin and Miller in transcribing from the fascicle manuscript version, and is in agreement with their readings.

2 *Bobolink* Species of blackbird native to the Americas.

3 This poem appears in Johnson as Poem 697; in Franklin as Poem 726; and in Miller as the second poem in Sheet 4 of Fascicle 35, page 364. The present text is in complete accord with the transcriptions of Franklin and Miller; it may be worth noting, however, that the mark at the end of line 5 could plausibly be read as a period.

4 *Odors* I.e., fragrant ointments or perfumes; *St Domingo* While "Santo Domingo" is the name of the capital city of the Dominican Republic, it is more likely that Dickinson means to refer to the newly independent Haiti, which had been known as Saint-Domingue under the French colonial regime. The Haitian Revolution of the late eighteenth century had been led by a coalition of free and enslaved black Haitians, resulting in the abolition of slavery and the expulsion of most white colonials from the country. To many white Americans in the nineteenth century, "Domingo" remained shorthand both for Haiti itself and for the violence of revolution (though the success of the Haitian Revolution also remained an inspiration to many black abolitionists).

5 *Colors* I.e., pigments or dyes; *Vera Cruz* State in Mexico, located on the coast of the Gulf of Mexico.

6 *Berries* Here likely referring to melons, which botanically speaking are a type of berry.

7 *Dower* Dowry; money brought by a bride into her marriage.

8 *Bobadilo* Francisco de Bobadilla, Spanish-born governor of the colony of Saint-Domingue (1499–1502).

9 This poem appears in Johnson as Poem 709; in Franklin as Poem 788; and in Miller as the second poem in Sheet 5 of Fascicle 37, pages 386–87. The present text is in complete accord with the transcriptions of Johnson, Franklin, and Miller; it may be noted, however, that the mark at the end of line 7 could plausibly be read as a right-slanting comma.

In the Parcel – Be the Merchant
Of the Heavenly Grace –
15 But reduce no Human Spirit
To Disgrace of Price –
—1863

[*Truth – is as old as God –*][1]

Truth – is as old as God –
His Twin identity
And will endure as long as He
A Co-Eternity –

5 And perish on the Day
Himself is borne away
From Mansion of the Universe
A lifeless Deity.
—1864, 1865

[*I never saw a Moor –*][2]

I never saw a Moor –
I never saw the Sea –
Yet know I how the Heather looks
And what a Billow[3] be.

5 I never spoke with God
Nor visited in Heaven –
Yet certain am I of the spot
As if the Checks[4] were given –
—1864

[*Color – Caste – Denomination –*][5]

Color – Caste – Denomination –
These – are Time's Affair –
Death's diviner Classifying
Does not know they are –

5 As in sleep – All Hue forgotten –
Tenets – put behind –
Death's large – Democratic fingers
Rub away the Brand.[6]

If Circassian[7] – He is careless –
10 If He put away
Chrysalis of Blonde – or Umber –
Equal Butterfly –

They emerge from His Obscuring –
What Death – knows so well –
15 Our minuter intuitions –
Deem unplausible
—1864

---

[1] This poem appears in Johnson as Poem 836; in Franklin as Poem 795; and in Miller under "Unbound Sheets," page 447. The version here is that which Dickinson retained, and is believed to date from 1865; the transcription here is entirely in accord with those of Johnson, Franklin, and Miller. Dickinson sent a variant to Josiah Holland in 1864; the latter is more heavily punctuated, with a dash (or, arguably, a right-slanting comma) after "identity," a comma after "perish," and dashes after "He" and "Universe."

[2] This poem appears in Johnson as Poem 1052; in Franklin as Poem 800; and in Miller under "Loose Poems," page 532. The present text is in agreement with the transcriptions of Johnson, Franklin, and Miller.

[3] *Billow* Wave.

[4] *Checks* Train tickets.

---

[5] This poem appears in Johnson as Poem 970; in Franklin as Poem 836; and in Miller as the first poem in Sheet 6 of Fascicle 40, page 412. The present text is in agreement with the transcriptions of Johnson, Franklin, and Miller except in one particular; we read the mark at the end of line 8 as a period rather than a dash. (It may also be worth noting that the mark at the end of the first line could plausibly be read as a right-slanting comma.) Dickinson provides one variant word choice in the manuscript: "incredible" for "unplausible" in the final line.

[6] *Brand* Physical identifying mark, possibly with reference to a brand burned into the skin of an enslaved person.

[7] *Circassian* Of Circassia, a region in the North Caucasus in what is now southwestern Russia.

[*She rose to His Requirement – dropt*][1]

She rose to His Requirement – dropt
The Playthings of Her Life
To take the honorable Work
Of Woman, and of Wife –

5 If ought[2] She missed in Her new Day,
Of Amplitude, or Awe –
Or first Prospective – Or the Gold
In using, wear away,

It lay unmentioned – as the Sea
10 Develope Pearl, and Weed,
But Only to Himself – be known
The Fathoms they abide –
—1864

[*The Poets light but Lamps*   ][3]

The Poets light but Lamps –
Themselves – go out –
The Wicks they stimulate
If vital Light

5 Inhere as do the Suns –
Each Age a Lens
Disseminating their
Circumference –
—1865

[*A Man may make a Remark –*][4]

A Man may make a Remark –
In itself – a quiet thing
That may furnish the Fuse unto a Spark
In dormant nature – lain –

5 Let us divide – with skill –
Let us discourse – with care –
Powder exists in Charcoal –
Before it exists in Fire.
—1865

[*Banish Air from Air –*][5]

Banish Air from Air –
Divide Light if you dare –
They'll meet
While Cubes in a Drop
5 Or Pellets of Shape
Fit.
Films[6] cannot annul
Odors return whole
Force Flame
10 And with a Blonde push
Over your impotence
Flits Steam.
—1865

---

1 This poem appears in Johnson as Poem 732; in Franklin as Poem 857; and in Miller as part of Fascicle 38, Sheet 4, pages 393–94. The present transcription of the manuscript is in agreement with those of Franklin and Miller—though it may be noted that the marks at the end of line 6 and after "unmentioned" in line 9 could plausibly be read as right-slanting commas.

     The poem was published under the title "The Wife" in Todd and Higginson's *Poems* (1890); in that version "Develops" is substituted for "Develope" in line 10 and "is" for "be" in line 11.

2 *ought* Aught.

3 This poem appears in Johnson as Poem 883; in Franklin as Poem 930; and in Miller under "Unbound Sheets," as the first poem on Sheet 15, page 436. The present transcription of the manuscript is in agreement with those of Franklin and Miller; Johnson reads the mark at the end of line 3 as a dash, but it seems more plausible to read it as the crossing of the final "t" in "stimulate."

4 This poem appears in Johnson as Poem 952; in Franklin as Poem 913; and in Miller under "Unbound Sheets," page 430. Except in taking the small mark at the end of the final line to be a period (as does Johnson) rather than a dash, the present text is in agreement with the transcriptions of Franklin and Miller. Dickinson provides alternative readings in every line except the fourth.

5 This poem appears in Johnson as Poem 854; in Franklin as Poem 963; and in Miller under "Unbound Sheets," pages 446–47. Editors differ over the transcription of the mark after "Fit"; Franklin and Miller transcribe it as a dash rather than a period.

6 *Films* In the sense of thin coverings.

[*As imperceptibly as Grief*]¹

As imperceptibly as Grief
The Summer lapsed away –
Too imperceptible at last
To feel like Perfidy² –

5   A Quietness distilled –
As Twilight long begun –
Or Nature – spending with Herself
Sequestered Afternoon –

Sobriety inhered
10   Though gaudy influence
The Maple lent unto the Road
And graphic Consequence

Invested sombre place –
As suddenly be worn
15   By sober Individual
A Homogeneous Gown –

Departed was the Bird –
And scarcely had the Hill
A flower to help His straightened face
20   In stress of Burial –

The Winds came closer up –
The Cricket spoke so clear
Presumption was – His Ancestors
Inherited the Floor –

25   The Dusk drew earlier in –
The Morning foreign shone –
The courteous – but harrowing Grace
Of Guest who would be gone –

And thus, without a Wing
30   Or Service of a Keel –
Our Summer made Her light Escape
Unto the Beautiful –
—c. 1865

[*The Heart has narrow Banks*]³

The Heart has narrow Banks
It measures like the Sea
In mighty – unremitting Bass
And Blue monotony

5   Till Hurricane bisect
And as itself discerns
Its insufficient Area
The Heart convulsive learns

That Calm is but a Wall
10   Of Unattempted Gauze
An instant's Push demolishes
A Questioning – dissolves.
—c. 1865

---

1   This poem appears in Johnson as Poem 1540; in Franklin as Poem 935; and in Miller as the first poem in Sheet 16 of "Unbound Sheets," page 437. A variant version includes only the first eight and the final eight lines, without any stanza breaks. The present text is in agreement with the transcriptions of Franklin and Miller—though it may be noted that the marks following "distilled" in line 5, "begun" in line 6, "courteous" in line 27, and "Keel" in line 30 could all plausibly be read as forward-slanting commas. Dickinson provides one alternative in the manuscript—"into" for "Unto" in the final line.

2   *Perfidy*   Treachery.

---

3   This poem appears in Johnson as Poem 928; in Franklin as Poem 960; and in Miller as the second poem of Sheet 21 in "Unbound Sheets," page 445. The present text, like those of Miller and Johnson, emends "It's" to "Its" in line 7. We agree with both Miller and Franklin in reading "monotony" in line 4 as lower case and "Unattempted" in line 10 as upper case (whereas Johnson reads the words as "Monotony" and "unattempted"). Dickinson provides one variant word choice in the manuscript—"paces" for "measures" in line 2.

[*Could I but ride indefinite*][1]

Could I but ride indefinite
As doth the Meadow Bee
And visit only where I liked
And no one visit me

5 And flirt all Day with Buttercups[2]
And marry whom I may
And dwell a little everywhere
Or better, run away

With no Police to follow
10 Or chase Him if He do
Till He should jump Peninsulas
To get away from me –

I said "But just to be a Bee"
Upon a Raft of Air
15 And row in Nowhere all Day long
And anchor "off the Bar"

What Liberty! So Captives deem
Who tight in Dungeons are.
—c. 1865

[*As the Starved Maelstrom laps the Navies*][3]

As the Starved Maelstrom[4] laps the Navies
As the Vulture teazed
Forces the Broods[5] in lonely Valleys
As the Tiger eased

5 By but a Crumb of Blood, fasts Scarlet
Till he meet a Man
Dainty adorned with Veins and Tissues
And partakes – his Tongue

Cooled by the Morsel for a moment
10 Grows a fiercer thing
Till he esteem his Dates and Cocoa
A Nutrition mean

I, of a finer Famine
Deem my Supper dry
15 For but a Berry of Domingo[6]
And a Torrid[7] Eye.
—1865

---

[3] This poem appears in Johnson as Poem 872; in Franklin as Poem 1064; and in Miller as the second poem in Sheet 45, under "Unbound Sheets," page 477. The present text is in agreement with the transcriptions of Johnson, Franklin, and Miller except in two particulars; we side with Franklin and Miller in retaining Dickinson's archaic variant spelling of "teazed," and with Johnson in reading the mark at the end of the poem as a period rather than a dash (though either reading is certainly defensible).

[4] *Maelstrom* Whirlpool.

[5] *Forces* I.e., overpowers; *Broods* Young birds.

[6] *Berry* In this context, a melon; *Domingo* Possibly a reference to Santo Domingo, the capital city of the Dominican Republic, but more likely to Saint-Domingue, the colonial name of Haiti prior to the 1791 Haitian Revolution, which had been led by free and enslaved black Haitians. Throughout the nineteenth century, "Domingo" remained common shorthand (especially to white Americans) both for Haiti itself and for the violence of revolution.

[7] *Torrid* Hot; also possibly a reference to the torrid zone, another name for the Tropics.

---

[1] This poem appears in Johnson as Poem 661; in Franklin as Poem 1056; and in Miller as the first poem in Sheet 43 under "Unbound Sheets," page 474. The present text is in agreement with the transcriptions of Franklin and Miller except in one particular; like Miller, we emend "Opon" to "Upon" in line 14.

[2] See overleaf for a buttercup from Dickinson's herbarium. (See also page 25 above.)

Ranunculus acris. 12-13.

A buttercup (from Dickinson's *Herbarium*—see page 25 above).

Seq. 32 from Dickinson's *Herbarium*, 1839–46. The flowers on the page depicted here include *Solanum tuberosum* (the potato flower; upper left), *Veronica serpyllifolia* (thyme-leaved speedwell; middle row, second from left), and *Digitalis purpurea* (common foxglove; upper right).

[*A narrow Fellow in the Grass*]

This poem was first published on 14 February 1866, in the *Springfield Republican*, a newspaper edited by Dickinson's friend Samuel Bowles. Dickinson did not submit the poem for publication, however; it has been plausibly conjectured that Susan Dickinson passed along to Bowles a now-lost manuscript copy which Dickinson had given her. A facsimile of the 1865 manuscript page appears on the facing page, followed by a transcription. Next appears the 1866 published version, and finally a transcription of the 1872 manuscript version.

This is the only known instance in which Dickinson complained of any of the specifics relating to the publication of one of her poems; in a 17 March 1866 letter to Higginson she commented as follows on the publication of the poem in the *Springfield Republican* (it is presumed that she enclosed a clipping of the newspaper's printed version with her letter):

> Lest you meet my Snake and suppose I deceive it was robbed of me—defeated too of the third line by the punctuation. The third and fourth were one—I had told you I did not print—I feared you might think me ostensible.[1] If I still entreat you to teach me, are you much displeased?

As is often the case with Dickinson's letters, it is difficult to be entirely clear of her meaning here. She does not want Higginson to think that she has deceived him—presumably in her protestations that she has not sought to have her work printed; she assures him that this poem was stolen from her. She asserts too that her intentions were "defeated" by the punctuation of the third line in the newspaper version, which retains the dash in the middle of the line but adds a question mark at the end of the line—whereas in the 1865 manuscript Dickinson has no punctuation. (Interestingly, Dickinson herself includes a question mark in her 1872 manuscript version—but in the middle of the line, not at its end.) On that point her complaint seems clear—but what does she mean by "The third and fourth were one"? Could she mean that the third and fourth [lines of the poem] were [intended to be set out as] one [line]? That would mean a line like this—

You may have met Him – did you not His notice sudden is –

which seems highly implausible. The alternative is that she means that the third and fourth [lines of the poem] were [wrongly made into] one [by the newspaper editors], when Dickinson herself had intended them to be separate lines—in other words, that Dickinson had intended the first stanza to have five lines. That appears to be how she writes the stanza in the 1872 version she sent to Susan Dickinson, in which she capitalizes the first letter of Did. With Dickinson it is frequently difficult to be sure of her intentions regarding line breaks, given that she so often capitalized words in the middle of lines, but in the 1872 version it seems clear that there would have been ample room on the page for Dickinson to write the word "Did," after "him?" if she had intended "You may have met him? Did you not" to form just one line. But here again, it is impossible to be entirely sure of Dickinson's intentions.

---

[1] *ostensible* Seeking visibility; ostentatious.

88-13

V

A narrow Fellow in
the Grass
Occasionally rides -
You may have met Him -
Did you not -
His notice sudden is -

The Grass divides as
with a Comb -
A spotted shaft is
seen -
And then it Closes
at your feet -
And opens further On -

He likes a Boggy
Acre
A Floor too Cool
for Corn
Yet when a Boy, and
Barefoot -

[*A narrow Fellow in the Grass*][1]

A narrow Fellow in the Grass
Occasionally rides –
You may have met Him – did you not
His notice sudden is –

5 The Grass divides as with a Comb –
A spotted shaft is seen –
And then it closes at your feet
And opens further on –

He likes a Boggy Acre
10 A Floor too cool for Corn
Yet when a Boy, and Barefoot –
I more than once at Noon

Have passed, I thought, a Whip lash
Unbraiding in the Sun
15 When stooping to secure it
It wrinkled, and was gone –

Several of Nature's People
I know, and they know me –
I feel for them a transport[2]
20 Of cordiality –

But never met this Fellow
Attended, or alone
Without a tighter breathing
And Zero at the Bone –
    —1865

THE SNAKE.

A narrow fellow in the grass
Occasionally rides;
You may have met him—did you not?
His notice instant is,
The grass divides as with a comb,
A spotted shaft is seen,
And then it closes at your feet,
And opens further on.

He likes a boggy acre,
A floor too cool for corn,
Yet when a boy and barefoot,
I more than once at noon
Have passed, I thought, a whip-lash,
Unbraiding in the sun,
When stooping to secure it,
It wrinkled and was gone.

Several of nature's people
I know, and they know me;
I feel for them a transport
Of cordiality.
Yet never met this fellow,
Attended or alone,
Without a tighter breathing,
And zero at the bone.

---

1   This poem appears in Johnson as Poem 986; in Franklin as Poem 1096; and in Miller as part of Unbound Sheet 54, pages 489–90. There are two manuscript versions extant; the first dates from 1865, while the second is included in an 1872 letter to Susan Dickinson. Johnson and Miller transcribe from the 1865 version; the two differ only slightly (the first two lines of the third stanza are punctuated differently, with Miller reading a dash at the end of the first line and Johnson reading a dash at the end of the second line). The image in the righthand column shows the version printed under the title "The Snake" in the *Springfield Republican* on 14 February 1866.

2   *transport*   Rush of emotion.

[*A narrow Fellow in the Grass*]

A narrow Fellow in the Grass
Occasionally rides –
You may have met him?
Did you not
His notice instant is –

The Grass divides as with a Comb –
A spotted Shaft is seen,
And then it closes at your Feet
And opens further on –

He likes a Boggy Acre –
A Floor too cool for Corn –
But when a Boy and Barefoot
I more than once at Noon

Have passed I thought a Whip Lash
Unbraiding in the Sun
When stooping to secure it
It wrinkled
And was gone –

Several of Nature's People
I know and they know me
I feel for them a transport
Of Cordiality

But never met this Fellow
Attended or alone
Without a tighter Breathing
And Zero at the Bone.
—1872

[*The Bustle in a House*]¹

The Bustle in a House
The Morning after Death
Is solemnest of industries
Enacted upon Earth –

The Sweeping up the Heart
And putting Love away
We shall not want to use again
Until Eternity –
—1865

[*A Spider sewed at Night*]²

A Spider sewed at Night
Without a Light
Upon an Arc of White –

If Ruff it was of Dame
Or Shroud of Gnome
Himself himself inform –

Of Immortality
His strategy
Was physiognomy³ –
—1868

---

1   This poem appears in Johnson as Poem 1078; in Franklin as Poem 1108; and in Miller as the third poem in Sheet 57, under "Unbound Sheets," page 494. The present text is in agreement with the transcriptions of Johnson, Franklin, and Miller except in one particular; we side with Franklin and Miller in reading the mark at the end of the poem as a dash rather than (as Johnson reads it) a period.

2   This poem appears in Johnson as Poem 1138; in Franklin as Poem 1163; and in Miller under "Poems Not Retained," pages 705–06. The present text is in agreement with the transcriptions of Franklin and Miller except in one particular; like Miller, we emend "Opon" to "Upon" in line 3. The dashes in the manuscript sent to Susan Dickinson very much resemble commas.

3   *physiognomy* Study of facial features to determine a person's character.

372

Tell all the truth"
but tell it slant –
Success in Circuit
lies
Too bright for our
word

infirm delight
the truth's superb
surprise
As Lightning to
the Children eased
with explanation kind
the truth must
dazzle gradually
moderately
Or every   man be
blind –

The manuscript of "Tell all the Truth but tell it slant" (Amherst College, Amherst–Amherst Manuscript # 372–Tell all the truth but tell it slant–asc:12240–p. 1). Dickinson's handwriting varied considerably both from one manuscript to another and over time.

[*Tell all the Truth but tell it slant –*][1]

Tell all the Truth but tell it slant –
Success in Circuit lies
Too bright for our infirm Delight
The Truth's superb surprise
5 As Lightning to the Children eased
With explanation kind
The Truth must dazzle gradually
Or every man be blind –
—1872

[*To pile like Thunder to its close*][2]

To pile like Thunder to its close
Then crumble grand away
While Everything created hid
This – would be Poetry –

5 Or Love – the two coeval[3] come –
We both and neither prove –
Experience either and consume –
For None see God and live –
—c. 1875

[*Apparently with no surprise*][4]

Apparently with no surprise
To any happy Flower
The Frost beheads it at its play –
In accidental power –
5 The blonde Assassin passes on –
The Sun proceeds unmoved
To measure off another Day
For an Approving God –
—c. 1884

[*A Word made Flesh is seldom*][5]

A Word made Flesh[6] is seldom
And tremblingly partook
Nor then perhaps reported
But have I not mistook
5 Each one of us has tasted
With ecstasies of stealth
The very food debated
To our specific strength –

A Word that breathes distinctly
10 Has not the power to die
Cohesive as the Spirit
It may expire if He –

---

1   This poem appears in Johnson as Poem 1129; in Franklin as Poem 1263; and in Miller under "Loose Poems," pages 563–64. The present transcription of the manuscript is in complete agreement with those of Johnson, Franklin, and Miller. Dickinson provides two variant word choices in the manuscript: "bold" for "bright" in line 3, and "moderately" for "gradually" in line 7.

2   This poem appears in Johnson as Poem 1247; in Franklin as Poem 1353; and in Miller under "Poems Not Retained," page 713. The present text is in agreement with the transcriptions of Franklin and Miller except in one particular; like Miller, we emend "it's" to "its" in line 1.

3   *coeval*   Of contemporaneous duration or existence.

4   This poem appears in Johnson as Poem 1624; in Franklin as Poem 1668; and in Miller under "Loose Poems," page 654. The present text is in agreement with the transcriptions of Johnson, Franklin, and Miller except in two particulars; like Johnson and Miller, we emend "it's" to "its" in line 3, and like Franklin and Miller we read the mark at the end of the poem as a dash rather than a period. Todd and Higginson edited the poem for *Poems* (1890), giving it the title "Death and Life."

5   This poem appears in Johnson as Poem 1651; in Franklin as Poem 1715; and in Miller under "Poems Transcribed by Others," page 671. No Dickinson manuscript appears to have survived, and the date of composition is not known; a transcription by Susan Dickinson has survived, and the poem appears in *Poems: Third Series* (1896). Johnson reads the manuscript as having three stanzas rather than two (with a stanza break after "He –").

6   *A Word made Flesh*   See John 1.1–14: "In the beginning was the Word, and the Word was with God, and the Word was God. ... And the Word was made flesh, and dwelt among us (and we beheld his glory, the glory as of the only begotten of the Father), full of grace and truth."

"Made Flesh and dwelt among us"
Could condescension be
15 Like this consent of Language
This loved Philology
—DATE OF COMPOSITION UNKNOWN (FIRST PUBLISHED
1896)

[*My life closed twice before its close;*][1]

My life closed twice before its close;
It yet remains to see
If Immortality unveil
A third event to me,

5 So huge, so hopeless to conceive
As these that twice befell.
Parting is all we know of heaven,
And all we need of hell.
—DATE OF COMPOSITION UNKNOWN (FIRST PUBLISHED
1896)

[*To make a prairie it takes a clover and one
bee,*][2]

To make a prairie it takes a clover and one bee,
One clover, and a bee,
And revery.
The revery alone will do,
5 If bees are few.
—DATE OF COMPOSITION UNKNOWN (FIRST PUBLISHED
1896)

---

[1]   This poem appears in Johnson as Poem 1732; in Franklin as Poem 1773; and in Miller under "Poems Transcribed by Others," page 686. No Dickinson manuscript appears to have survived; a transcription by Mabel Todd has survived, and the poem appears in *Poems: Third Series* (1896). Franklin retains the spelling "it's" in line 1.

[2]   This poem appears in Johnson as Poem 1755; in Franklin as Poem 1779; and in Miller under "Poems Transcribed by Others," page 688. No Dickinson manuscript appears to have survived; a transcription by Mabel Todd has survived, and the poem appears in *Poems: Third Series* (1896).

Fascicle 13

In 1858 Dickinson began organizing manuscript copies of her poems into groups (later called "fascicles"), which she sewed together by hand.

Though the fascicles were later broken up, the research of R.W. Franklin and Cristanne Miller has made it possible to reconstruct the order in which the poems were presented in these fascicles. Franklin orders the poems chronologically in his edition, whereas Miller's edition of the poems takes the fascicles as its first principle of organization.

Presented below are the texts of all the poems in Dickinson's Fascicle 13. Since all sheets of the fascicle have been dated to early 1862, that date is not repeated for each individual poem. Nor are the poems given their first lines as titles; in this as in other respects, the aim here is to give students a sense of the way in which Dickinson brought groups of poems together and preserved them. Typically, Dickinson indicated breaks between poems with wavy lines, which we have attempted to reproduce here.

I know some lonely Houses off the Road[1]
A Robber'd like the look of –
Wooden barred,
And Windows hanging low,
5 Inviting to –
A Portico,
Where two could creep –
One – hand the Tools –
The other peep –
10 To make sure all's asleep –
Old fashioned eyes –
Not easy to surprise!

How orderly the Kitchen'd look, by night –
With just a Clock –

15 But they could gag the Tick –
And Mice won't bark –
And so the Walls – don't tell –
None – will –

A pair of Spectacles ajar just stir –
20 An Almanac's aware –
Was it the Mat – winked,
Or a nervous Star?
The Moon – slides down the stair,
To see who's there!

25 There's plunder – where –
Tankard, or Spoon –
Earring – or Stone –
A Watch – Some Ancient Brooch
To match the Grandmama –
30 Staid sleeping – there –

Day – rattles – too –
Stealth's – slow –
The Sun has got as far
As the third Sycamore –
35 Screams Chanticleer[2]
"Who's there"?

And Echoes – Trains away,
Sneer – "Where"!
While the old Couple, just astir,
40 Fancy[3] the Sunrise – left the door ajar!

I can wade Grief –[4]
Whole Pools of it –
I'm used to that –
But the least push of Joy
5 Breaks up my feet –
And I tip – drunken –

---

[1] This poem appears in Johnson as Poem 289; in Franklin as Poem 311; and in Miller as the first poem in Sheet 1 of Fascicle 13, pages 148–49. The present transcription follows Johnson rather than Miller and Franklin in reading the mark after "stair" at the end of line 23 as a comma rather than a dash. Following Miller and Franklin we read "all's asleep" as lower case, whereas Johnson reads both words as capitalized. Following Johnson and Miller rather than Franklin, we emend "wont" to "won't" in line 16 and "dont" to "don't" in line 17.

    The poem appears in Todd and Higginson's *Poems* (1890); they assign to it the title "The Lonely House."

[2] *Chanticleer* In fables, the name conventionally given to a rooster.

[3] *Fancy* Imagine that.

[4] This poem appears in Johnson as Poem 250; in Franklin as Poem 352; and in Miller as the second poem in Fascicle 13, page 149. The present transcription is in accord with those of all three—including in the transcription of the mark that appears at the end of line 5 as a dash; it could as easily be read as a right-slanting comma.

Let no Pebble – smile –
'Twas the New Liquor –
That was all!

10   Power is only Pain –
Stranded – thro' Discipline,
Till Weights – will hang –
Give Balm – to Giants –
And they'll wilt, like Men –
15   Give Himmaleh[1] –
They'll carry – Him!

You see I cannot see – your lifetime –[2]
I must guess –
How many times it ache for me – today – Confess –
How many times for my far sake
5   The brave eyes film –
But I guess guessing hurts –
Mine – get so dim!

Too vague – the face –
My own – so patient – covets –
10   Too far – the strength –
My timidness enfolds –
Haunting the Heart –
Like her translated faces –
Teasing the want –
15   It – only – can suffice!

"Hope" is the thing with feathers –[3]
That perches in the soul –
And sings the tune without the words –
And never stops – at all –

5   And sweetest – in the Gale – is heard –
And sore must be the storm –
That could abash the little Bird
That kept so many warm –

I've heard it in the chilliest land
10   And on the strangest Sea –
Yet, never, in Extremity,
It asked a crumb – of Me.

To die – takes just a little while –[4]
They say it doesn't hurt –
It's only fainter – by degrees –
And then – it's out of sight –
5   A darker Ribbon – for a Day –
A Crape[5] upon the Hat –
And then the pretty sunshine comes –
And helps us to forget –
The absent – mystic – creature –
10   That but for love of us –
Had gone to sleep – that soundest time –
Without the weariness –

---

[1]   *Give Himmaleh*   I.e., Give [them] a mountain. ("Himmaleh" is a now obsolete spelling of "Himalaya.")

[2]   This poem appears in Johnson as Poem 253; in Franklin as Poem 313; and in Miller as the first poem in Sheet 2 of Fascicle 13, pages 149–50. The present transcription follows Johnson in emending "Teazing" to "Teasing" in line 14; in other respects it agrees with that of all three editors—though it may be noted that the marks that appear at the ends of lines 10 and 12 could both be plausibly read as right-slanting commas.

[3]   This poem appears in Johnson as Poem 254; in Franklin as Poem 314; and in Miller within Fascicle 13, Sheet 2, page 150. All three of those editors punctuate the poem identically, in the same way it is punctuated here (and on page 30 above). Alternative readings are certainly possible in lines 6, 11, and 12, and perhaps line 4 as well.

[4]   This poem appears in Johnson as Poem 255; in Franklin as Poem 315; and in Miller as the third poem of the second sheet of Fascicle 13, pages 150–51. The present transcription follows Johnson and Miller in emending "does'nt" to "doesn't" in line 2 and "opon" to "upon" in line 6; Franklin leaves both uncorrected.

[5]   *Crape*   Fabric typically dyed black and used for mourning garments.

If I'm lost – now –[1]
That I was found –
Shall still my transport[2] be –
That once – on me – those Jasper Gates[3]
5   Blazed open – suddenly –

That in my awkward – gazing – face –
The Angels – softly peered –
And touched me with their fleeces,
Almost as if they cared –
10 I'm banished – now – you know it –
How foreign that can be –
You'll know – Sir – when the Savior's face
Turns so – away from you –

Delight is as the flight –[4]
Or in the Ratio of it,
As the Schools would say –
The Rainbow's way –
5   A Skein[5]
Flung colored, after Rain,
Would suit as bright,
Except that flight
Were Aliment –

10 "If it would last"
I asked the East,
When that Bent Stripe
Struck up my childish
Firmament[6] –
15 And I, for glee,

Took Rainbows, as the common way,
And empty skies
The Eccentricity –

And so with Lives –
20 And so with Butterflies –
Seen magic – through the fright
That they will cheat the sight –
And Dower[7] latitudes far on –
Some sudden morn –
25 Our portion – in the fashion –
Done –

She sweeps with many-colored Brooms –[8]
And leaves the shreds behind –
Oh Housewife in the Evening West –
Come back – and – dust the Pond!

5   You dropped a Purple Ravelling in –
You dropped an Amber thread –
And now you've littered all the East
With Duds of Emerald!

And still, she plies[9] her spotted Brooms –
10 And still the Aprons fly,
Till Brooms fade softly into stars –
And then I come away –

---

[1]   This poem appears in Johnson as Poem 256; in Franklin as Poem 316; and in Miller as the first poem in Sheet 3 of Fascicle 13. The present transcription is in accord with those of all three.

[2]   *transport*   Overwhelming emotion, especially joy.

[3]   *Jasper Gates*   In Revelation 21 the precious stone jasper is mentioned repeatedly as one of the building materials of the heavenly city.

[4]   This poem appears in Johnson as Poem 257; in Franklin as Poem 317; and in Miller as the fourth and last poem of Sheet 2 in Fascicle 13. With the exception of Johnson's decision to capitalize "skies" in line 17, modern editors agree regarding the transcription of the poem.

[5]   *Skein*   Thread or yarn twisted into a bundle.

[6]   *Firmament*   Sky or heavens.

[7]   *Dower*   While the present editors have retained Dickinson's spelling, it seems probable that she here intended "dour"—meaning "bleak" or "gloomy."

[8]   This poem appears in Johnson as Poem 219; in Franklin as Poem 318; and in Miller as the second poem of Sheet 3, Fascicle 13, page 152. The present editors follow conventional practice in transcribing punctuation here, but the poem is a good example of the degree to which the convention of representing all of Dickinson's dashes in the same fashion has the effect of flattening very substantial differences. In this case, the marks at the ends of each of the following lines have the appearance of right-slanting commas: lines 1, 3, 5, 6, 9, and 11.

[9]   *plies*   Uses; works with.

Of Bronze – and Blaze –[1]
The North – Tonight –
So adequate – it forms –
So preconcerted with itself –
5   So distant – to alarms –
An Unconcern so sovreign
To Universe, or me –
Infects my simple spirit
With Taints of Majesty –
10   Till I take vaster attitudes –
And strut upon my stem –
Disdaining Men, and Oxygen,
For Arrogance of them –

My Splendors, are Menagerie –
15   But their Competeless Show
Will entertain the Centuries
When I, am long ago,
An Island in dishonored Grass –
Whom none but Beetles – Daisies, know –

There's a certain Slant of light,[2]
Winter Afternoons –
That oppresses, like the Heft
Of Cathedral Tunes –

5   Heavenly Hurt, it gives us –
We can find no scar,
But internal difference –
Where the Meanings, are –

None may teach it – Any –
10   'Tis the Seal Despair –
An imperial affliction
Sent us of the Air –

When it comes, the Landscape listens –
Shadows – hold their breath –
15   When it goes, 'tis like the Distance
On the look of Death –

Blazing in Gold – and[3]
Quenching – in Purple!
Leaping – like Leopards in the sky –
Then – at the feet of the old Horizon –
5   Laying its spotted face – to die!

Stooping as low as the kitchen window –
Touching the Roof –
And tinting the Barn –
Kissing its Bonnet to the Meadow –
10   And the Juggler of Day – is gone!

---

[1]   This poem appears in Johnson as Poem 290; in Franklin as Poem 319; and in Miller as the third poem in Sheet 3 of Fascicle 13, pages 152–53. Dickinson's manuscript includes three variants: "manners" as an alternative to "attitudes" in line 10; "Some" as an alternative to "An" in line 18; and "Beetles" as an alternative to "Daisies" in the final line. The present editors follow Johnson in reading "Tonight" in line 2, and follow both Johnson and Miller in emending "opon" to "upon" in line 11. The transcription of punctuation is in agreement with that of Franklin and Miller—though it may be noted that the marks that appear after "Bronze" in line 1 and after "Grass" in line 18 could both be plausibly read as right-slanting commas.

The poem appears in Todd and Higginson's *Poems: Third Series* (1896); they assign to it the title "Aurora."

[2]   This poem appears in Johnson as Poem 258; in Franklin as Poem 320; and in Miller as the fourth poem in Sheet 3, Fascicle 13, page 153. The present transcription is in accordance with the principles established by Johnson, Franklin, and Miller; both Franklin and Miller read the poem as having thirteen dashes. (Johnson reads the mark after "difference" as a comma; in other respects his transcription is identical to those of Franklin and Miller.)

Todd and Higginson include the poem in their edition of *Poems* (1890), with "weight" replacing "heft" in line 3, and with only one dash.

[3]   This poem appears in Johnson as Poem 228; in Franklin as Poem 321; and in Miller as the first poem in Sheet 4 of Fascicle 13, pages 153–54. The present editors have followed Johnson and Miller in emending "it's" to "its" in line 5 and again in line 9 (whereas Franklin leaves them uncorrected). The dashes in this poem are quite regular in their shape and placing; there are no significant issues in their transcription.

Good Night! Which put the Candle out?[1]
A jealous Zephyr[2] – not a doubt –
Ah, friend, you little knew
How long at that celestial wick
5 The Angels – labored diligent –
Extinguished – now – for you!

It might – have been the Light House spark –
Some Sailor – rowing in the Dark –
Had importuned to see!
10 It might – have been the Waning lamp
That lit the Drummer from the Camp
To purer Reveille![3]

⸻

Read – Sweet – how others – strove –[4]
Till we – are stouter –
What they – renounced –
Till we – are less afraid –
5 How many times they – bore the faithful witness –
Till we – are helped
As if a Kingdom – cared!

Read then – of faith –
That shone above the fagot[5] –
10 Clear strains of Hymn
The River could not drown –
Brave names of Men –
And Celestial Women –
Passed out – of Record
15 Into – Renown!

Put up my lute![6]
What of – my Music!
Since the sole ear I cared to charm –
Passive – as Granite – laps my music –
5 Sobbing – will suit – as well as psalm!

Would but the "Memnon"[7] of the Desert –
Teach me the strain
That vanquished Him –
When He – surrendered to the Sunrise –
10 Maybe – that – would awaken – them!

⸻

There came a Day – at Summer's full –[8]
Entirely for me –
I thought that such – were for the Saints –
When Resurrections – be –

5 The Sun – as common – went abroad –
The Flowers   accustomed – blew –
As if no Soul the Solstice passed –
That maketh all things new.

The time was scarce profaned – by speech –
10 The symbol of a word
Was needless – as at Sacrament –
The Wardrobe – of Our Lord –

---

1 This poem appears in Johnson as Poem 259; in Franklin as Poem 322; and in Miller as the second poem in Sheet 4 of Fascicle 13, page 154. There are no significant transcription issues.

2 *Zephyr* Personification of a gentle wind.

3 *Reveille* Morning drum beat or bugle call to wake troops.

4 This poem appears in Johnson as Poem 260; in Franklin as Poem 323; and in Miller as the third poem in Sheet 4 of Fascicle 13, page 154. There are few transcription issues—though the mark after "drown" at the end of line 11 could easily be read as a right-slanting comma.

5 *fagot* Literally, a bundle of twigs used to make a fire; sometimes used to indicate the punishment of heretics, in reference to the practice of burning them alive.

6 This poem appears in Johnson as Poem 261; in Franklin as Poem 324; and in Miller as the fourth poem of Sheet 4 in Fascicle 13, page 155. There are no significant transcription issues.

7 *Memnon* In ancient Greece, Memnon was a Trojan warrior famed for singing to his mother at sunrise. When a large Egyptian statue sustained damage in 27 BCE, it began at sunrise to often emit an almost musical sound; the statue was then given the name Memnon.

8 This poem appears in Johnson as Poem 322; in Franklin as Poem 325; and in Miller as the first poem in Sheet 5 of Fascicle 13, pages 155–56. There are several crossings-out and alternatives provided in the manuscript; of these the most significant is "Revelations" as an alternative for "Resurrections" in line 4. The present editors follow Miller in representing with italics the emphasis that Dickinson gives, by underlining, to the word "that" in the second-last line.

Each was to each – the sealed church –
Permitted to commune – this time –
15 Lest we too awkward – show –
At "Supper of the Lamb."[1]

The hours slid fast – as hours will –
Clutched tight – by greedy hands –
So – faces on two Decks – look back –
20 Bound to opposing Lands –

And so – when all the time had failed –
Without external sound –
Each – bound the other's Crucifix –
We gave no other bond –

25 Sufficient troth[2] – that we shall rise –
Deposed – at length – the Grave –
To *that* New Marriage –
Justified – through Calvaries[3] of Love!

The lonesome for they know not What –[4]
The Eastern Exiles – be –
Who strayed beyond the Amber line
Some madder Holiday –

5 And ever since – the purple Moat
They strive to climb – in vain –
As Birds – that tumble from the clouds
Do fumble at the strain –

The Blessed Ether – taught them –
10 Some Transatlantic Morn –
When Heaven – was too common – to miss –
Too sure – to dote upon!

How the old Mountains drip with Sunset[5]
How the Hemlocks burn –
How the Dun Brake[6] is draped in Cinder
By the Wizard Sun –

5 How the old Steeples hand the Scarlet
Till the Ball is full –
Have I the lip of the Flamingo
That I dare to tell?

Then, how the Fire ebbs like Billows –
10 Touching all the Grass
With a departing – Sapphire – feature –
As a Duchess passed –

How a small Dusk crawls on the Village
Till the Houses blot
15 And the odd Flambeau,[7] no men carry
Glimmer on the Street –

How it is Night – in Nest and Kennel –
And where was the Wood –
Just a Dome of Abyss is Bowing
20 Into Solitude –

These are the Visions flitted Guido –
Titian – never told –
Domenichino[8] dropped his pencil –
Paralyzed, with Gold –

---

[1]   *Supper of the Lamb*   See Revelation 19.9: "And he saith unto me, Write, Blessed are they which are called unto the marriage supper of the Lamb." The phrase refers to the Eucharist held in Heaven after the second coming of Christ (who is symbolized by a lamb).

[2]   *troth*   Promise or pledge.

[3]   *Calvaries*   Suffering; with reference to Calvary, the site of Christ's crucifixion.

[4]   This poem appears in Johnson as Poem 262; in Franklin as Poem 326; and in Miller as the last poem in Sheet 5 of Fascicle 13, page 156. Like both Johnson and Miller, we emend "opon" to "upon" in the final line.

[5]   This poem appears in Johnson as Poem 291; in Franklin as Poem 327; and in Miller as the first poem in Sheet 6 of Fascicle 13, pages 156–57. The present transcription is in accord with those of Franklin and Miller, though it may be noted that the marks at the ends of lines 9, 11, 17, 18, and 23 could all plausibly be read as right-slanting commas.

[6]   *Dun Brake*   Greenish-brown fern.

[7]   *Flambeau*   Torch.

[8]   *Guido … Domenichino*   Guido Reni (1575–1642), Titian (1488–1576), and Domenichino (1581–1641), well-known Italian artists of the late Renaissance.

Of Tribulation, these are They,[1]
Denoted by the White[2] –
The Spangled Gowns, a lesser Rank
Of Victors – designate –

5 All these – did Conquer –
But the ones who overcame most times –
Wear nothing commoner than snow –
No Ornament, but Palms –

Surrender – is a sort unknown –
10 On this superior soil –
Defeat – an outgrown Anguish –
Remembered, as the Mile

Our panting Ankle barely passed –
When Night devoured the Road –
15 But we – stood whispering in the House –
And all we said – was "Saved"!

If your Nerve, deny you –[3]
Go above your Nerve –
He can lean against the Grave,
If he fear to swerve –

5 That's a steady posture –
Never any bend
Held of those Brass arms –
Best Giant made –

If your Soul stagger seesaw –
10 Lift the Flesh door –
The Poltroon[4] wants Oxygen –
Nothing more –
—1862

---

1   This poem appears in Johnson as Poem 325; in Franklin as Poem
328; and in Miller as the second poem in Sheet 6 of Fascicle 13, page
157. The present editors correct one misspelling, emending "Ancle"
to "Ankle." In other respects the transcription here is in accord with
those of Franklin and Miller—though it may be noted that the
marks at the ends of lines 6, 7, 11, and 13 could all plausibly be read
as right-slanting commas.

2   *Of Tribulation ... the White*   In Revelation 7 and 12 people who
have emerged from "great tribulation" are described as being "arrayed
in white robes."

3   This poem appears in Johnson as Poem 292; in Franklin as Poem
329; and in Miller as the third and final poem in Sheet 6 of Fascicle
13, page 158. The present transcription is in accord with those of
Franklin and Miller—though it may be noted that the marks at the
ends of lines 5, 9, and 11 could all plausibly be read as right-slanting
commas.

4   *Poltroon*   Weak, unheroic person.

SELECTED LETTERS

Dickinson's Personal Correspondence

In addition to having written roughly 1800 poems, Emily Dickinson was a keen and expressive letter writer, and her personal correspondence includes letters written to at least one hundred recipients. Among these were former classmates such as Abiah Root (later Abiah Strong) and Jane Humphrey; friends Otis Lord and Samuel Bowles, the former a judge and the latter the editor of the *Springfield Republican*; and Susan Gilbert Dickinson, the wife of Dickinson's brother Austin, to whom Dickinson wrote hundreds of letters. Many of these letters, especially those sent to Susan, contained versions of Dickinson's poems; included below is an exchange in which Susan advises the poet on how to refine the poem that begins "Safe in their Alabaster Chambers." Another frequent correspondent, from Dickinson's first soliciting his opinion on her poetry in 1862, was Thomas Wentworth Higginson, a leading figure in American intellectual life through much of the second half of the nineteenth century; Higginson's essay "Emily Dickinson's Letters" appears in this volume on pages 93–110.

Of continual fascination to many readers of Dickinson's correspondence are a set of three extant letters, likely part of a larger correspondence of which the remainder has been lost, written between approximately 1858 and 1861 to an unknown recipient Dickinson repeatedly addresses as "Master." Numerous identities have been posited by scholars for this mystery recipient, including Otis Lord and Samuel Bowles, but these remain purely speculative; some have suggested that the "Master" was not a real person at all, but rather an aspect of an imaginative exercise. It is not known whether the letters that have survived were ever actually posted, though their condition—with numerous words scribbled out and inserted in the margins—suggests that these were only drafts. One of Dickinson's "Master" letters is included below.

To Abiah Root

[29 January 1850]

Very dear Abiah.

The folks have all gone away—they thought that they left me alone, and contrived things to amuse me should they stay long, and *I* be lonely. Lonely indeed—they did'nt look, and they could'nt have seen if they had, who should bear me company. *Three* here instead of *one*—would'nt it scare them? A curious trio, part earthly and part spiritual two of us—the other all heaven, and no earth. *God* is sitting here, looking into my very soul to see if I think right tho'ts. Yet I am not afraid, for I try to be right and good, and he knows every one of my struggles. He looks very gloriously, and everything bright seems dull beside him, and I dont dare to look directly at him for fear I shall die. Then *you* are here—dressed in that quiet black gown and cap—that funny little cap I used to laugh at you about, and you dont appear to be thinking about anything in particular, not in one of your *breaking dish* moods I take it, you seem aware that I'm writing you, and are amused I should think at any such friendly manifestation when you are already present. *Success* however even in making a fool of one's self is'nt to be despised, so I shall persist in writing, and you may in laughing at me, if you are fully aware of the value of time as regards your immortal spirit, I cant say that I advise you to laugh, but if you are punished, and I warned you, that can be no business of mine. So I fold up my arms, and leave you to fate—may it deal very kindly with you! The trinity winds up with me, as you may have surmised, and I certainly would'nt be at the fag end[1] but for civility to you. This selfsacrificing spirit will be the ruin of me! I am occupied principally with a cold just now, and the dear creature *will* have so much attention that my time slips away amazingly. It has heard *so* much of New Englanders, of their kind attentions to strangers, that it's come all the way from the Alps to determine the truth of the tale—it says the half was'nt told it, and I begin to be afraid it was'nt. Only think, came all the way from that distant Switzerland to find what was the truth! Neither husband—protector—nor friend accompanied it, and so utter a state of loneliness gives friends if nothing else. You are dying of curiosity, let me arrange that pillow to make your exit easier! I stayed at home all Saturday afternoon, and treated some disagreeable people who insisted upon calling here as tolerably as I could—when evening shades began to fall, I turned upon my heel, and walked. Attracted by the gaiety visible in the street I still kept walking till a little creature pounced upon a

---

[1]   *fag end* I.e., the end of the list.

thin shawl I wore, and commenced riding—I stopped, and begged the creature to alight, as I was fatigued already, and quite unable to assist others. It would'nt get down, and commenced talking to itself—"cant be New England—must have made some mistake, disappointed in my reception, dont agree with accounts, Oh what a world of deception, and fraud—Marm,[1] will [you] tell me the name of this country—it's Asia Minor,[2] is'nt it. I intended to stop in New England." By this time I was so completely exhausted that I made no farther effort to rid me of my load, and travelled home at a moderate jog, paying no attention whatever to it, got into the house, threw off both bonnet, and shawl, and out flew my tormentor, and putting both arms around my neck began to kiss me immoderately, and express so much love, it completely bewildered me. Since then it has slept in my bed, eaten from my plate, lived with me everywhere, and will tag me through life for all I know. I think I'll wake first, and get out of bed, and leave it, but early, or late, it is dressed before me, and sits on the side of the bed looking right into my face with such a comical expression it almost makes me laugh in spite of myself. I cant call it interesting, but it certainly *is* curious—has two peculiarities which would quite win your heart, a huge pocket-handkerchief, and a very red nose. The first seems so very *abundant*, it gives you the idea of independence, and prosperity in business. The last brings up the "jovial bowl,[3] my boys," and such an association's worth the having. If it *ever* gets tired of *me*, I will forward it to *you*—you would love it for *my* sake, if not for it's own; it will tell you some queer stories about me—how I sneezed so loud one night that the family thought the last trump[4] was sounding, and climbed into the currant-bushes to get out of the way—how the rest of the people arrayed in long night-gowns folded their arms, and were waiting—but this is a wicked story, it can tell some *better* ones. Now my dear friend, let me tell you that these last thoughts are fictions—vain imaginations to lead astray foolish young women. They are flowers of speech,

they both *make*, and *tell* deliberate falsehoods, avoid them as the snake, and turn aside as from the *Bottle* snake,[5] and I dont *think* you will be harmed. Honestly tho', a snake-bite is a serious matter, and there cant be too much said, or done about it. The big serpent bites the deepest, and we get so accustomed to it's bites that we dont mind about them. "Verily I say unto you fear *him*."[6] Wont you read some work upon snakes— I have a real anxiety for you! *I* love those little green ones that slide around by your shoes in the grass—and make it rustle with their elbows—they are rather my favorites on the whole, but I would'nt influence *you* for the world! There is an air of misanthropy about the striped snake that will commend itself at once to your taste, there is no monotony about it—but we will more of this again. Something besides severe colds, and serpents, and we will try to find *that* something. It cant be a garden, can it, or a strawberry bed, which rather belongs to a garden—nor it cant be a school-house, nor an Attorney at Law. Oh dear I dont know *what* it is! Love for the absent dont *sound* like it, but try it, and see how it goes.

I miss you very much indeed, think of you at night when the world's nodding, "nidnid nodding"—think of you in the daytime when the cares of the world, and it's toils, and it's continual vexations choke up the love for friends in some of our hearts; remember your warnings sometimes—try to do as you told me sometimes—and sometimes conclude it's no use to try; then my heart says it *is*, and new trial is followed by disappointment again. I wondered when you had gone why we did'nt talk more—it was'nt for want of a subject, it never *could be* for *that*. Too many perhaps, such a crowd of people that nobody heard the speaker, and all went away discontented. You astounded me in the outset— perplexed me in the continuance—and wound up in a grand snarl—I shall be all my pilgrimage unravelling. Rather a dismal prospect certainly—but "it's always the darkest the hour before day," and this earlier sunset promises an earlier rise—a sun in splendor—and glory, flying out of it's purple nest. Would'nt you love to see

---

[1] *Marm*   Ma'am.

[2] *Asia Minor*   Roughly, modern-day Turkey.

[3] *jovial bowl*   I.e., a bowl of punch or other alcoholic drink shared at gatherings—which might make its drinkers' noses red.

[4] *the last trump*   The last of the seven trumpets expected to announce the apocalypse, as described in the Book of Revelations.

---

[5] *Bottle snake*   In her edition of Dickinson's letters, Mabel Loomis Todd corrected this to "rattle-snake."

[6] *Verily ... fear him*   See Luke 12.5: "But I will forewarn you whom ye shall fear: Fear him, which after he hath killed hath power to cast into hell; yea, I say unto you, Fear him."

God's bird, when it first tries it's wings? If you were here I would tell you something—*several* somethings which have happed since you went away, but time, and space, as usual, oppose themselves, and I put my treasures away till "we *two* meet again."[1] The hope that I shall continue in love towards you—and *vice versa* will sustain me till then. If you are thinking soon to go away, and to show your face no more, just inform me—will you—I would have the "long lingering look" which you cast behind—It would be an invaluable addition to my treasures, and "keep your memory green."[2] "Lord keep all our memories green," and help on our affection, and tie "the link that doth us bind"[3] in a tight bow-knot that will keep it from separation, and stop us from growing old, if *that* is impossible— make old age pleasant to us—put it's arms around us kindly, and when we go home—let that home be called *Heaven*!

Your very sincere, and *wicked* friend,

Emily E. Dickinson. ...[4]

To Jane Humphrey

[3 April 1850]

Jane, *dear* Jane.

The voice of *love* I heeded, tho' *seeming* not to; the voice of affliction is louder, more earnest, and needs it's friends, and they know this need, and put on their wings of affection, and fly towards the lone one, and sing, sing sad music, but there's something sustaining in it. Your *first* words found me far out in the world, crowding, and hurrying, and busying, the last ones

have found me there, but I have struggled with some success, and am free to be with you a little. Trouble is with you, and trial, and your spirit is sorely cumbered, and I can hardly dare to talk, *earthly* things seem faded, and fallen; could I speak with a right of Heaven, and the Savior, and "rest for the weary"[5] I know I could bring strength to you, and could lift you above this cumbering; but I can tell you how dearly I love you, if *this* will make you happier. I have been much with you since you first wrote me, *always* with you, but *more* since *then*, for the last few days you have been *very* near, very dear *indeed*, and I have wished, and prayed to *see* you, and to *hear* you, and to feel your warm heart beating near me, what music in such quiet ticking! You mourn Jennie, how does it *seem* to mourn, you *watch*, and the lamp is waning, where is your spirit resting, have you any dear friend to be near you, and to tell you of peace? It would be very precious to *me* to do so, to be a strong arm you might lean on when you looked all around, and could find none, this is none of it permitted now, and I think, and strive, and attempt but come no nearer the end.

Can I console so far off, wont the comfort waste in conveying, and be *not*, when my letter gets there? How long had your father been sick, and why hav'nt you told me before, we have *certainly* loved one another! How very much you have suffered, and I hav'nt known anything about it, but supposed you away in Warren, teaching, and thinking of home, and *sometimes* of us, and a place we wish *was* your home. I have dreamed of you, and talked of you, and wished for you, and have almost thought I should see you, it has seemed that some way would help me, and a providence would bring you, and yet you have not come, and I am so very tired of waiting. Some one said you would come in vacation, and I looked towards it very eagerly, made my treasures ready against it, and prepared my mind, and heart to welcome you in so kindly, and disappointment put a great cloud in my sky, and it's so high I cannot reach it, and it's doing a deal of harm. How lonely this world is growing, something so desolate creeps over the spirit and we dont know it's name, and it wont go away, either Heaven is

---

[1] *we two meet again* See Shakespeare's *Macbeth* 1.1.1: "When shall we three meet again?" Spoken by one of the three witches in reference to their regular gatherings.

[2] *keep your memory green* Phrase repeated several times in Charles Dickens's Christmas story "The Haunted Man" (1848).

[3] *the link that doth us bind* See "The Definition of Love" by Andrew Marvell (1621–78): "Therefore the love which us doth bind, / But Fate so enviously debars, / Is the conjunction of the mind, / And opposition of the stars."

[4] ... In this case, as with several others of the letters included here, Dickinson appends a post-script in which she discusses news of mutual friends, local details, etc.

[5] *rest for the weary* See Matthew 11.28–30: "Come unto me, all ye that labour and are heavy laden, and I will give you rest. Take my yoke upon you, and learn of me; for I am meek and lowly in heart: and ye shall find rest unto your souls. For my yoke is easy, and my burden is light."

seeming greater, or Earth a great deal more small, or God is more "Our Father," and we feel our need increased. Christ is calling everyone here, all my companions have answered, even my darling Vinnie believes she loves, and trusts him, and I am standing alone in rebellion, and growing very careless. Abby, Mary, Jane, and farthest of all my Vinnie have been seeking, and they all believe they have found; I cant tell you *what* they have found, but *they* think it is something precious. I wonder if it *is*? How strange is this sanctification, that works such a marvellous change, that sows in such corruption, and rises in golden glory, that brings Christ down, and shews him, and lets him select his friends! In the day time it seems like Sundays, and I wait for the bell to ring, and at evening a great deal stranger, the "still small voice" grows earnest and rings, and returns, and lingers, and the faces of good men shine, and bright halos come around them; and the eyes of the disobedient look down, and become ashamed. It *certainly* comes from God—and I think to receive it is blessed—not that I know it from *me*, but from those on whom *change* has passed. They secm so very tranquil, and their voices are kind, and gentle, and the tears fill their eyes so often, I really think I envy them. You know all about John Sanford, and Thurston, and all the rest, and I cant say more about it. You must pray when the rest are sleeping, that the hand may be held to me, and I may be led away.

How long does it seem since you left me, has the time been fleet, or lagging—been filled with hope, and the future, or waste, and a weary wilderness—and no one who knew the road? I would whisper to you in the evening of many, and curious things—and by the lamps eternal read your thoughts and response in your face, and find what you thought about me, and what I have done, and am doing; I know you would be surprised, whether in pleasure, or disappointment it does'nt become me to say—I have dared to do strange things—bold things, and have asked no advice from any—I have heeded beautiful tempters, yet do not think I am wrong. Oh I have needed my trusty Jane—my friend encourager, and sincere counciller, my rock, and strong assister! I could make you tremble for me, and be very much afraid, and wonder how things would end—Oh Jennie, it would relieve me to tell you all, to sit down at your feet, and look in your eyes, and confess what *you only* shall know, an experience bitter,

and sweet, but the sweet did so beguile me—and life has had an aim, and the world has been too precious for your poor—and striving sister! The winter was all one dream, and the spring has not yet waked me, I would *always* sleep, and dream, and it never should turn to morning, so long as night is so blessed. What do you weave from all these threads, for I know you hav'nt been idle the while I've been speaking to you, bring it nearer the window, and I will see, it's all wrong unless it has one gold thread in it, a long, big shining fibre which hides the others—and which will fade away into Heaven while you hold it, and from there come back to me. I hope belief is not wicked, and assurance, and perfect trust—and a kind of twilight feeling before the moon is seen—I hope human nature has truth in it—Oh I pray it may not deceive—confide—cherish, have a great faith in—do you dream from all this what I mean? Nobody *thinks* of the joy, nobody *guesses* it, to all appearance old things are engrossing, and new ones are not revealed, but there *now* is nothing old, things are budding, and springing, and singing, and you rather think you are in a green grove, and it's branches that go, and come. I shall see you *sometime* darling, and that sometime *may* not be distant, try to grow fast, and live really, and endure, and wait in patience—and reward *cannot* be distant. Be strong Jennie in remembrance, dont let "bygones be bygones"—love what you are taken from, and cherish us tho, so dim. Dont put us in narrow graves—we shall *certainly rise* if you do, and scare you most prodigiously, and carry you off perhaps! "This is the end of the earth."

Very affectionately your friend

Emily E. Dickinson.

To Abiah Root

[7 and 17 May 1850]

Dear Remembered.

The circumstances under which I write you this morning are at once glorious, afflicting, and beneficial—glorious in *ends*, afflicting in *means*, and *beneficial* in *trust* in *both*. Twin loaves of bread have just been born into the world under my auspices—fine children—the image of their *mother*—and *here* my dear friend is the *glory*.

On the lounge asleep, lies my sick mother, suffering intensely from Acute Neuralgia—except at a moment like this, when kind sleep draws near, and beguiles her, *here* is the *affliction*.

I need not draw the *beneficial* inference—the good I myself derive, the winning the spirit of the patience the genial house-keeping influence stealing over my mind, and soul, you know all these things I would say, and will seem to suppose they are *written*, when indeed they are only *thought*. On Sunday my mother was taken, had been perfectly well before, and could remember no possible imprudence which should have induced the disease, everything has been done, and tho' we think her gradually throwing it off, she still has much suffering. I have always neglected the culinary arts, but attend to them now from necessity, and from a desire to make everything pleasant for father, and Austin. Sickness makes desolation, and "the day is dark, and dreary,"[1] but health will come back I hope, and light hearts, and smiling faces. We are sick hardly ever at home, and dont know what to do when it comes, wrinkle our little brows, and stamp our little feet, and our tiny souls get angry, and command it to go away. Mrs *Brown* will be glad to see it, old-ladies *expect* to die, as for *us*, the young, and the active, with all longings "for the strife," *we* to "perish by the road-side, weary with the march of life"[2] no-no my dear "Father Mortality," get out of our way if you please, we will call if we ever want you, Good-morning Sir, ah Good-morning! When I am not at work in the kitchen, I sit by the side of mother, provide for her little wants—and try to cheer, and encourage her. I ought to be glad, and grateful that I *can* do anything now, but I do feel so very lonely, and so anxious to have her cured. I hav'nt repined but *once*, and you shall know all the why. While I washed dishes at noon in that little "sink-room" of our's, I heard a well-known rap, and a friend I love *so* dearly came and asked me to ride in the woods, the sweet-still woods, and I wanted to exceedingly—I told him I could not go, and he said he was disappointed—he wanted me very much—then the tears came into my eyes, tho' I tried to choke them back, and he said I *could*, and *should* go, and it seemed to me unjust. Oh I struggled with great temptation, and it cost me much of denial, but I think in the end I conquered, not a glorious victory Abiah, where you hear the rolling drum, but a kind of a helpless victory, where triumph would come of itself, faintest music, weary soldiers, nor a waving flag, nor a long-loud shout. I had read of Christ's temptations, and how they were like our own, only he did'nt sin; I wondered if *one* was like mine, and whether it made him angry—I couldnt make up my mind; do you think he ever did?

I went cheerfully round my work, humming a little air till mother had gone to sleep, then cried with all my might, seemed to think I was much abused, that this wicked world was unworthy such devoted, and terrible sufferings, and came to my various senses in great dudgeon at life, and time, and love for affliction, and anguish.

What shall we do my darling, when trial grows more, and more, when the dim, lone light expires, and it's dark, so very dark, and we wander, and know not where, and cannot get out of the forest—whose is the hand to help us, and to lead, and forever guide us, they talk of a "Jesus of Nazareth," will you tell me if it be he?

I presume you have heard from Abby, and know what she now believes—she makes a sweet, girl christian, religion makes her face quite different, calmer, but full of radiance, holy, yet very joyful. She talks of herself quite freely, seems to love Lord Christ most dearly, and to wonder, and be bewildered, at the life she has always led. It all looks black, and distant, and God, and Heaven are near, she is certainly very much changed.

She has told you about things here, how the "still small voice" is calling, and how the people are listening, and believing, and truly obeying—how the place is very solemn, and sacred, and the bad ones slink away, and are sorrowful—not at their wicked lives—but at this strange time, great change. *I* am one of the lingering *bad* ones, and so do *I* slink away, and pause,

---

[1]   *the day ... and dreary* See Henry Wadsworth Longfellow's poem "The Rainy Day" (1842): "The day is cold, and dark, and dreary" (line 1).

[2]   *for the strife ... march of life* See Longfellow's poem "Footsteps of the Angels" (1839): "He, the young and strong, who cherished / Noble longings for the strife, / By the roadside fell and perished, / Weary with the march of life!" (13–16).

and ponder, and ponder, and pause, and do work without knowing why—not surely for *this* brief world, and more sure it is not for Heaven—and I ask what this message *means* that they ask for so very eagerly, *you* know of this depth, and fulness, will you *try* to tell me about it?

It's *Friday* my dear Abiah, and that in another week, yet my mission is unfulfilled—and you so sadly neglected, and dont know the reason why. Where do you think I've strayed, and from what new errand returned? I have come from "*to and fro*, and walking up, and down"[1] the same place that Satan hailed from, when God asked him where he'd been, but not to illustrate further I tell you I have been dreaming, dreaming a *golden* dream, with eyes all the while wide open, and I guess it's almost morning, and besides I have been at work, providing the "food that perisheth,"[2] scaring the timorous dust, and being obedient, and kind. *I* call it kind obedience in the books the Shadows write in, it may have another name. I am yet the Queen of the court, if regalia be dust, and dirt, have three loyal subjects, whom I'd rather relieve from service. Mother is still an invalid tho' a partially restored one—Father and Austin still clamor for food, and I, like a martyr am feeding them. Would'nt you love to see me in these bonds of great despair, looking around my kitchen, and praying for kind deliverance, and declaring my "Omar's beard" I never was in such plight. *My* kitchen I think I called it, God forbid that it was, or shall be my own—God keep me from what they call *households*, except that bright one of "faith"!

Dont be afraid of my imprecations, they never did anyone harm, and they make me feel so cool, and so very much more comfortable!

Where are you now Abiah, where are your thoughts, and aspirings, where are your young affections, not with the *boots*, and *whiskers*; any with *me* ungrateful, *any* tho' dropping, dying? I presume you are loving your mother, and loving the stranger, and wandered,

visiting the poor, and afflicted, and reaping whole fields of blessings. Save me a *little* sheaf—only a very little one! Remember, and care for me sometimes, and scatter a fragrant flower in this wilderness life of mine by writing me, and by not forgetting, and by lingering longer in prayer, that the Father may bless one more!

Your aff friend,

Emily.

To Susan Gilbert Dickinson

[April 1852]

Sunday afternoon

So sweet and still, and Thee, Oh Susie, what need I more, to make my heaven whole?

Sweet Hour, blessed Hour, to carry me to you, and to bring you back to me, long enough to snatch one kiss, and whisper Good bye, again.

I have thought of it all day, Susie, and I fear of but little else, and when I was gone to meeting[3] it filled my mind so full, I could not find a *chink* to put the worthy pastor; when he said "Our Heavenly Father," I said "Oh Darling Sue"; when he read the 100th Psalm, I kept saying your precious letter all over to myself, and Susie, when they sang—it would have made you laugh to hear one little voice, piping to the departed. I made up words and kept singing how I loved you, and you had gone, while all the rest of the choir were singing Hallelujahs. I presume nobody heard me, because I sang *so small*, but it was a kind of a comfort to think I might put them out, singing of you. I a'nt there this afternoon, tho', because I am here, writing a little letter to my dear Sue, and I am very happy. I think of ten weeks—Dear One, and I think of love, and you, and my heart grows full and warm, and my breath stands still. The sun does'nt shine at all, but I can feel a sunshine stealing into my soul and making it all summer, and every thorn, a *rose*. And I pray that such summer's sun shine on my Absent One, and cause her bird to sing!

---

[1]   *to and fro ... and down*   See Job 2.2: "And the Lord said unto Satan, From whence comest thou? And Satan answered the Lord, and said, From going to and fro in the earth, and from walking up and down in it."

[2]   *food that perisheth*   See John 6.27: "Labour not for the meat which perisheth, but for that meat which endureth unto everlasting life, which the Son of man shall give unto you: for him hath God the Father sealed."

---

[3]   *meeting*   I.e., church.

You have been happy, Susie, and now are sad—and the whole world seems lone; but it wont be so always, "some days *must* be dark and dreary"![1] You wont cry any more, will you, Susie, for my father will be your father, and my home will be your home,[2] and where you go, I will go, and we will lie side by side in the kirkyard.[3]

I have parents on earth, dear Susie, but your's are in the skies, and I have an earthly fireside, but you have one above, and you have a "Father in Heaven," where I have *none*—and a *sister* in heaven, and I know they love you dearly, and think of you every day.

Oh I wish I had half so many dear friends as you in heaven—I could'nt spare them now—but to know they had got there safely, and should suffer nevermore—Dear Susie!

I know I was very naughty to write such fretful things, and I know I could have helped it, if I had tried hard enough, but I thought my heart would break, and I knew of nobody here that cared anything about it—so I said to myself, "We will tell Susie about it." You dont know what a comfort it was, and you wont know, till the big cup of bitterness is filled brimfull, and they say, "Susie, drink it!" Then Darling, let me be there, and let me drink the half, and you will feel it all!

I am glad you have rested, Susie. I wish the week had been *more*, a whole *score* of days and joys for you, yet again, had it lasted longer, then had you not come so soon and I had been lonelier, it is right as it is! Ten weeks, they will seem short to you—for care will fill them, but to Mattie and me, long. We shall grow tired, waiting, and our eyes will ache with looking for you, and with now and then a tear. And yet we have *hope* left, and we shall keep her busy, cheering away the time. Only think Susie, it is vacation now—there shall be no more vacation until ten weeks have gone, and no more snow; and how very little while it will be now, before you and I are sitting out on the broad stone step, mingling our lives together! I cant talk of it now tho', for it makes me long and yearn so, that I cannot sleep tonight, for thinking of it, and you.

Yes, we did go sugaring,[4] and remembered who was gone—and who was there last year, and love and recollection brought with them Little Regret, and set her in the midst of us.

Dear Susie, Dear Joseph;[5] why take the best and dearest, and leave our hearts behind? While the Lovers sighed; and twined oak leaves, and the *anti* enamored ate sugar, and crackers, in the house, I went to see what I could find. Only think of it, Susie; I had'nt any appetite, nor any Lover, either, so I made the best of fate, and gathered antique stones, and your little flowers of moss opened their lips and spoke to me, so I was not alone, and bye and bye Mattie and me might have been seen sitting together upon a high—gray rock, and we might have been heard talking, were anyone very near! And did thoughts of that dear Susie go with us on the rock, and sit there 'tween us twain?[6] Loved One, thou knowest!

I gathered something for you, because you were not there, an acorn, and some moss blossoms, and a little shell of a snail, so whitened by the snow you would think 'twas a cunning artist had carved it from alabaster—then I tied them all up in a leaf with some last summer's grass I found by a brookside, and I'm keeping them all for you.

I saw Mattie at church today, tho' could not speak to her. Friday evening I saw her, and talked with her besides. Oh I do love her—and when you come if we all live till then, it will be *precious*, Susie. You speak to me of sorrow, of what you have "lost and loved,"[7] say rather, of what you have loved and *won*, for it is *much*, dear Susie; I can count the big, true hearts by *clusters*, full of bloom, and bloom amaranthine, because *eternal*! Emilie—

---

[1]   *some days ... and dreary*   See Longfellow's "The Rainy Day," line 15.

[2]   *my father ... your home*   Dickinson's brother, Austin Dickinson, had begun courting Susan Gilbert in 1850, and the two would become officially engaged in autumn 1853.

[3]   *where you go ... in the kirkyard*   See Ruth 1.16–17: "And Ruth said, Intreat me not to leave thee, or to return from following after thee; for whither thou goest, I will go; and where thou lodgest, I will lodge; thy people shall be my people, and thy God my God; Where thou diest, will I die, and there will I be buried: the Lord do so to me, and more also, if ought but death part thee and me"; *kirkyard*   Churchyard; graveyard.

[4]   *sugaring*   Collecting sap from maple trees in the early spring to boil down into syrup.

[5]   *Joseph*   Possible reference to Dickinson's friend Joseph Lyman (1829–72).

[6]   *'tween us twain*   Between the two of us.

[7]   *lost and loved*   See Alfred, Lord Tennyson's *In Memoriam* 27, lines 15–16: "'Tis better to have loved and lost / Than never to have loved at all" (1850).

To Susan Gilbert Dickinson

[27 June 1852]

Sunday afternoon—

My Susie's last request; yes, darling, I grant it, tho' few, and fleet the days which separate us now—but six more weary days, but six more twilight evens, and my lone little fireside, my *silent* fireside is once more full.

"We are seven, and one in heaven,"[1] we are *three* next Saturday, if I have *mine* and heaven has none.

Do not mistake, my Susie, and rather than the car, ride on the golden wings where you will ne'er come back again—do not forget the lane, and the little cot that stands by it, when people from the clouds will beckon you, and smile at you, to have you go with them—Oh Susie, my child, I sit here by my window, and look each little while down towards that golden gateway beneath the western trees, and I fancy I see you coming, you trip upon the green grass, and I hear the crackling leaf under your little shoe; I hide behind the chair, I think I will surprise you, I grow too eager to see you. I hasten to the door, and start to find me that you are not there. And very, very often when I have waked from sleep, *not quite* waked, I have been sure I saw you, and your dark eye beamed *on me* with such a look of tenderness that I could only weep, and bless God for you.

Susie, will you indeed come home next Saturday, and be my own again, and kiss me as you used to?

Shall I indeed behold you, not "darkly, but face to face"[2] or am I *fancying* so, and dreaming blessed dreams from which the day will wake me? I hope for you so much, and feel so eager for you, feel that I *cannot* wait, feel that *now* I must have you—that the expectation once more to see your face again, makes me feel hot and feverish, and my heart beats so fast—I go to sleep at night, and the first thing I know, I am sitting there wide awake, and clasping my hands tightly, and thinking of next Saturday, and "never a bit" of you.

Sometimes I must have Saturday before tomorrow comes, and I wonder if it w'd make any difference with God, to give it to me *today*, and I'll let him have Monday, to make him a Saturday; and then I feel so funnily, and wish the precious day would'nt come quite so soon, till I could know how to feel, and get my thoughts ready for it.

Why, Susie, it seems to me as if my absent Lover was coming home so soon—and my heart must be so busy, making ready for him.

While the minister this morning was giving an account of the Roman Catholic system, and announcing several facts which were usually startling, I was trying to make up my mind wh' of the two was prettiest to go and welcome you in, my fawn colored[3] dress, or my blue dress. Just as I had decided by all means to wear the blue, down came the minister's fist with a terrible rap on the counter, and Susie, it scared me so, I hav'nt got over it yet, but I'm glad I reached a conclusion! I walked home from meeting with Mattie, and *incidentally* quite, something was said of you—and I think one of us remarked that you would be here next Sunday; well—Susie—what it was I don't presume to know, but my gaiters[4] seemed to leave me, and I seemed to move on wings—and I move on wings now, Susie, on wings as white as snow, and as bright as the summer sunshine—because I am with you, and so few short days, you are with me at home. Be patient then, my Sister, for the hours will haste away, and Oh so soon!

Susie, I write most hastily, and very carelessly too, for it is time for me to get the supper, and my mother is gone and besides, my darling, so near I seem to you, that I *disdain* this pen, and wait for a *warmer* language. With Vinnie's love, and my love, I am once more

Your Emilie

---

[1]   *We are ... in heaven*   Reference to William Wordsworth's poem "We Are Seven," in which a "little cottage girl" insists to the narrator that there are seven children living in her home—even though two of them have died and gone to heaven.

[2]   *not ... face to face*   See 1 Corinthians 13.12: "For now we see through a glass, darkly; but then face to face."

---

[3]   *fawn colored*   Light brown or beige.

[4]   *gaiters*   Water resistant coverings worn over the shoes and lower legs.

To Samuel Bowles

[February 1861]

Dear friend.

You remember the little "Meeting"—we held for you—last spring? We met again—Saturday—'Twas May—when we "adjourned"—but then Adjourns—are all—The meetings wore alike—Mr. Bowles—The Topic—did not tire us—so we chose no new—We voted to remember you—so long as both should live—including Immortality. To count you as ourselves—except sometimes more tenderly—as now—when you are ill—and we—the haler[1] of the two—and so I bring the Bond—we sign so many times—for you to read, when Chaos comes—or Treason—or Decay—still witnessing for Morning.

We hope—it is a tri-Hope—composed of Vinnie's—Sue's—and mine—that you took no more pain—riding in the sleigh.

We hope our joy to see you give of its own degree to you. We pray for your new health—the prayer that goes not down—when they shut the church—We offer you our cups—stintless—as to the Bee—the Lily, her new Liquors—

> Would you like Summer? Taste of our's—
> Spices? Buy, here!
> Ill! We have Berries, for the parching!
> Weary! Furloughs of Down!
> Perplexed! Estates of Violet—Trouble ne'er
> looked on!
> Captive! We bring Reprieve of Roses!
> Fainting! Flasks of Air!
> Even for Death—a Fairy Medicine—
> But, which is it—Sir?

Emily.

To Unknown Recipient

[c. 1861]

Master.

If you saw a bullet hit a Bird—and he told you he was'nt shot—you might weep at his courtesy, but you would certainly doubt his word.

One drop more from the gash that stains your Daisy's[2] bosom—then would you believe? Thomas' faith in Anatomy, was stronger than his faith in faith.[3] God made me—Master[4]—I did'nt be—myself. I dont know how it was done. He built the heart in me—Bye and bye it outgrew me—and like the little mother—with the big child—I got tired holding him. I heard of a thing called "Redemption"—which rested men and women. You remember I asked you for it—you gave me something else. I forgot the Redemption[5] and was tired—no more—[6]I am older—tonight, Master but the love is the same—so are the moon and the crescent. If it had been God's will that I might breathe where you breathed—and find the place—myself—at night—if I can[7] never forget that I am not with you—and that sorrow and frost are nearer than I—if I wish with a might I cannot repress—that mine were the Queen's place—the love of the Plantagenet[8] is my only apology—To

---

2 *Daisy* Nickname used by Dickinson to refer to herself, solely in the context of the "Master" letters.

3 *Thomas' faith … in faith* Reference to Thomas the Apostle, or "Doubting Thomas;" who refused to believe that Jesus had been resurrected until he was able to touch his physical wounds; see John 20.24–29.

4 *Master* In the manuscript, this word replaces the scribbled-out word "Sir."

5 *Redemption* Immediately after this word, Dickinson crossed out the sentence: "in the Redeemed—I didn't tell you for a long time, but I knew you had altered me—I."

6 — Immediately after this dash, Dickinson crossed out the sentence: "so dear did this stranger become that were it, or my breath—the Alternative—I had tossed the fellow away with a smile."

7 *can* This word was inserted above the line.

8 *Plantagenet* Name of the royal family whose members ruled England from 1154 until their defeat during the Wars of the Roses in 1485.

---

1 *haler* Healthier; stronger.

come nearer than presbyteries[1]—and nearer than the new Coat—that the tailor made—the prank of the Heart at play on the Heart—in holy Holiday—is forbidden me—You make me say it over—I fear you laugh—when I do not see—[2]"Chillon"[3] is not funny. Have you the Heart in your breast—Sir—is it set like mine—a little to the left—has it the misgiving—if it wake in the night—perchance—itself to it—a timbrel[4] is it—itself to it a tune.

These things are holy,[5] Sir, I touch them hallowed,[6] but persons who pray—dare remark[7] "Father"! You say I do not tell you all—Daisy confessed—and denied not.

Vesuvious   dont   talk—Etna[8]—dont—[9]one   of them—said a syllable—a thousand years ago, and Pompeii heard it, and hid forever—She could'nt look the world in the face, afterward—I suppose—Bashfull Pompeii! "Tell you of the want"—you know what a leech is, dont you—and[10] Daisy's arm is small—and you have felt the horizon hav'nt you—and did the sea—never come so close as to make you dance?

I dont know what you can do for it—thank you— Master—but if I had the Beard on my cheek—like you—and you—had Daisy's petals—and you cared so for me—what would become of you? Could you forget me in fight, or flight—or the foreign land? Could'nt

Carlo,[11] and you and I walk in the meadows an hour— and nobody care but the Bobolink[12]—and his—silver scruple? I used to think when I died—I could see you— so I died as fast as I could—but the "Corporation"[13] are going Heaven too so[14] wont be sequestered—now[15] Say I may wait for you—say I need go with no stranger to the to me—untried[16] fold—I waited a long time— Master—but I can wait more—wait till my hazel hair is dappled—and you carry the cane—then I can look at my watch—and if the Day is too far declined—we can take the chances[17] for Heaven—What would you do with me if I came "in white?" Have you the little chest to put the Alive—in?

I want to see you more—Sir—than all I wish for in this world—and the wish—altered a little—will be my only one—for the skies.

Could you come to New England—[18]would you come to Amherst—Would you like to come—Master?

Would[19] Daisy disappoint you—no—she would'nt —Sir—it were comfort forever—just to look in your face, while you looked in mine—then I could play in the woods till Dark—till you take me where Sundown cannot find us—and the true keep coming—till the town is full.[20]

I did'nt think to tell you, you did'nt come to me "in white," nor ever told me why,

No Rose, yet felt myself a'bloom,
No Bird—yet rode in Ether.

---

[1]   *presbyteries*   Referring to the part of a church reserved for the members of the clergy who are leading services.

[2]   —   Immediately after this dash, Dickinson crossed out the word "but."

[3]   *Chillon*   Reference to the 1816 poem "The Prisoner of Chillon" by English Romantic poet Lord Byron.

[4]   *timbrel*   Tambourine.

[5]   *holy*   In the manuscript, this word replaces the crossed-out word "reverent."

[6]   *hallowed*   This word replaces the crossed-out word "reverently."

[7]   *remark*   Immediately after this word, Dickinson crossed out the word "our."

[8]   *Vesuvious … Etna*   Mount Vesuvius and Mount Etna are both volcanoes in Italy. Vesuvius famously erupted near the city of Pompeii in 79 CE, killing hundreds of people.

[9]   —   Immediately after this dash, Dickinson crossed out the word "Thy."

[10]   *and*   Immediately after this word, Dickinson crossed out the words "remember that."

[11]   *Carlo*   Dickinson's dog, a brown Newfoundland.

[12]   *Bobolink*   Blackbird native to North America, mentioned several times in Dickinson's poems and letters.

[13]   *Corporation*   Ruling body.

[14]   *so*   Immediately after this word, Dickinson crossed out the word "Eternity."

[15]   *now*   Immediately after this word, Dickinson crossed out the words "at all."

[16]   *untried*   Immediately after this word, Dickinson crossed out the word "country."

[17]   *chances*   Immediately after this word, Dickinson crossed out the word "of."

[18]   —   Immediately after this dash, Dickinson crossed out the words "this summer—could."

[19]   *Would*   Before this word, Dickinson crossed out the words "Would it do harm—yet we both fear God—"

[20]   *full*   At the end of this sentence, Dickinson crossed out the words "Will you tell me if you will?"

To Susan Gilbert Dickinson

[1861]

Safe in their Alabaster Chambers,
Untouched by morning—
And untouched by noon—
Lie the meek members of the Resurrection—
Rafter of Satin—and Roof of Stone—

Grand go the Years—in the Crescent—about them—
Worlds scoop their Arcs—
And Firmaments—row—
Diadems—drop—and Doges—surrender—
Soundless as dots—on a Disc of snow—

Perhaps this verse would please you better—Sue—

                                          Emily.

Susan Dickinson to Emily Dickinson

[1861]

I am not suited dear Emily with the second verse—It
is remarkable as the chain lightening that blinds us hot
nights in the Southern sky but it does not go with the
ghostly shimmer of the first verse as well as the other
one—It just occurs to me that the first verse is com-
plete in itself it needs no other, and can't be coupled—
Strange things always go alone—as there is only one
Gabriel[1] and one Sun—You never made a peer for that
verse, and I *guess* you[r] kingdom does'nt hold one—I
always go to the fire and get warm after thinking of
it, but I never *can* again—The flowers are sweet and
bright and look as if they would kiss one—ah, they
expect a humming-bird—Thanks for them of course—
and not thanks only recognition either—Did it ever
occur to you that is all there is here after all—"Lord
that I may receive my sight"[2]—

Susan is tired making bibs for her bird[3]—her ring-
dove—he will paint my cheeks when I am old to pay
me—

                                          Sue—

To Susan Gilbert Dickinson

[1861]

Is *this, frostier?*

Springs—shake the Sills—
But— the Echoes—stiffen—
Hoar—is the Window—and
Numb—the Door—
Tribes of Eclipse—in Tents of Marble—
Staples of Ages—have buckled—there—

Dear Sue—

Your praise is good—to me—because I *know* it
knows—and *suppose*—it *means*—
    Could I make you and Austin[4]—proud—some-
time—a great way off—'twould give me taller feet—
    Here is a crumb—for the "Ring dove"—and a spray
for *his Nest*, a little while ago—*just*—"*Sue.*"

                                          Emily.

To Thomas Wentworth Higginson

[15 April 1862]

Mr Higginson,

Are you too deeply occupied to say if my Verse is alive?
    The Mind is so near itself—it cannot see, dis-
tinctly—and I have none to ask—

---

1   *Gabriel* Archangel described in the Bible, who in the New
Testament visits the Virgin Mary to announce that she is pregnant
with Jesus.

2   *Lord … my sight* See Mark 10.51: "And Jesus answered and said
unto him, What wilt thou that I should do unto thee? The blind man

said unto him, Lord, that I might receive my sight."

3   *her bird* Possible reference to Susan's son Edward, who was
born in 1861.

4   *Austin* Susan's husband and Dickinson's brother, William
Austin Dickinson (1829–95).

Should you think it breathed—and had you the leisure to tell me, I should feel quick gratitude—

If I make the mistake—that you dared to tell me—would give me sincerer honor—toward you—

I enclose my name—asking you, if you please—Sir—to tell me what is true?

That you will not betray me—it is needless to ask—since Honor is it's own pawn—

To Thomas Wentworth Higginson

[25 April 1862]

Mr Higginson,

Your kindness claimed earlier gratitude—but I was ill—and write today, from my pillow.

Thank you for the surgery[1]—it was not so painful as I supposed. I bring you others—as you ask—though they might not differ—

While my thought is undressed—I can make the distinction, but when I put them in the Gown—they look alike, and numb.

You asked how old I was? I made no verse—but one or two—until this winter—Sir—

I had a terror—since September[2]—I could tell to none—and so I sing, as the Boy does by the Burying Ground—because I am afraid—You inquire my Books—For Poets—I have Keats[3]—and Mr and Mrs Browning.[4] For Prose—Mr Ruskin[5]—Sir Thomas Browne[6]—and the Revelations.[7] I went to school—

but in your manner of the phrase—had no education. When a little Girl, I had a friend, who taught me Immortality—but venturing too near, himself—he never returned—Soon after, my Tutor, died—and for several years, my Lexicon—was my only companion—Then I found one more—but he was not contented I be his scholar—so he left the Land.

You ask of my Companions Hills—Sir—and the Sundown—and a Dog—large as myself, that my Father bought me—They are better than Beings[8]—because they know—but do not tell—and the noise in the Pool, at Noon—excels my Piano. I have a Brother and Sister—My Mother does not care for thought—and Father, too busy with his Briefs[9]—to notice what we do—He buys me many Books—but begs me not to read them—because he fears they joggle the Mind. They[10] are religious—except me—and address an Eclipse, every morning—whom they call their "Father." But I fear my story fatigues you—I would like to learn—Could you tell me how to grow—or is it unconveyed—like Melody—or Witchcraft?

You speak of Mr Whitman[11]—I never read his Book—but was told that he was disgraceful—

I read Miss Prescott's "Circumstance,"[12] but it followed me, in the Dark—so I avoided her—

Two Editors of Journals came to my Father's House, this winter—and asked me for my Mind—and when I asked them "Why," they said I was penurious[13]—and they, would use it for the World—

I could not weigh myself—Myself—

My size felt small—to me—I read your Chapters in the Atlantic—and experienced honor for you—I was sure you would not reject a confiding question—

---

1   *surgery*   I.e., Higginson's critiques of the poems Dickinson had sent him with her previous letter.

2   *I had … since September*   It is unclear what "terror" Dickinson is referring to here, though biographers have posited a number of physical and psychological afflictions.

3   *Keats*   English Romantic poet John Keats (1795–1821).

4   *Mr and Mrs Browning*   Married English poets Robert and Elizabeth Barrett Browning (1812–89 and 1806–61, respectively).

5   *Mr Ruskin*   English art critic and philosopher John Ruskin (1819–1900).

6   *Sir Thomas Browne*   English scientist and theologian (1605–82).

7   *the Revelations*   Final book of the New Testament; Revelations is an esoteric and prophetic text which describes, among many things, the eventual second coming of Christ.

8   *Beings*   I.e., human beings.

9   *Briefs*   Legal documents (Dickinson's father was a lawyer).

10   *They*   I.e., Dickinson's parents and siblings.

11   *Mr Whitman*   Walt Whitman (1819–92), American poet. The first edition of his collection *Leaves of Grass* was published in 1855; it was well received by many but also scandalized a number of more conservative readers, who were troubled by what they saw as its obscenity as well as by its highly unconventional form.

12   *Circumstance*   Short story by American writer Harriet Elizabeth Prescott Spofford, published in *The Atlantic Monthly* in 1860; the story's unnamed female protagonist is pursued through the dark woods by a figure referred to as the "Indian Devil."

13   *penurious*   Poor.

Is this—Sir—what you asked me to tell you?

Your friend,
E—Dickinson.

To Thomas Wentworth Higginson

[7 June 1862]

Dear friend.

Your letter gave no Drunkenness, because I tasted Rum before—Domingo[1] comes but once—yet I have had few pleasures so deep as your opinion, and if I tried to thank you, my tears would block my tongue—

My dying Tutor told me that he would like to live till I had been a poet, but Death was much of Mob as I could master—then—And when far afterward—a sudden light on Orchards, or a new fashion in the wind troubled my attention—I felt a palsy,[2] here—the Verses just relieve—

Your second letter surprised me, and for a moment, swung—I had not supposed it. Your first—gave no dishonor, because the True—are not ashamed—I thanked you for your justice—but could not drop the Bells whose jingling cooled my Tramp—Perhaps the Balm, seemed better, because you bled me, first.

I smile when you suggest that I delay "to publish"—that being foreign to my thought, as Firmament to Fin[3]—If fame belonged to me, I could not escape her—if she did not, the longest day would pass me on the chase—and the approbation of my Dog, would forsake me—then—My Barefoot—Rank is better—

You think my gait "spasmodic"—I am in danger—Sir—

You think me "uncontrolled"—I have no Tribunal.

Would you have time to be the "friend" you should think I need? I have a little shape—it would not crowd your Desk—nor make much Racket as the Mouse, that dents your Galleries—

If I might bring you what I do—not so frequent to trouble you—and ask you if I told it clear—'twould be control, to me—

The Sailor cannot see the North—but knows the Needle[4] can—

The "hand you stretch me in the Dark," I put mine in, and turn away—I have no Saxon,[5] now—

As if I asked a common Alms,[6]
And in my wondering hand
A Stranger pressed a Kingdom,
And I, bewildered, stand—
As if I asked the Orient
Had it for me a Morn—
And it should lift it's purple Dikes,
And shatter me with Dawn!

But, will you be my Preceptor,[7] Mr Higginson?

Your friend
E Dickinson—

To Thomas Wentworth Higginson

[July 1862]

Could you believe me—without? I had no portrait, now,[8] but am small, like the Wren, and my Hair is bold, like the Chestnut Bur—and my eyes, like the Sherry in the Glass, that the Guest leaves—Would this do just as well?

---

[1] *Domingo* Dickinson may be referring either to the capital city of the Dominican Republic or to the country of Haiti (which had formerly been known as "Saint-Domingue"), for which "Domingo" remained common shorthand in the United States during the nineteenth century. "Domingo" often specifically referenced the Haitian Revolution of 1791, which had resulted in the abolition of slavery and in the expulsion of most French colonials from the country. Both Haiti and the Dominican Republic were (and are) prominent producers of rum.

[2] *palsy* Tremor or paralysis.

[3] *Firmament* The sky or heavens; *Fin* Fish.

[4] *Needle* I.e., the needle of a compass.

[5] *Saxon* I.e., the English language (which is largely derived from Anglo-Saxon); Dickinson may intend here to refer specifically to prose.

[6] *Alms* Charity.

[7] *Preceptor* Teacher.

[8] *Could you ... now* Only two confirmed likenesses of Dickinson are known to exist: a painting of her with her siblings at the age of about ten, and a daguerreotype taken when she was about sixteen.

It often alarms Father—He says Death might occur, and he has Molds[1] of all the rest—but has no Mold of me, but I noticed the Quick[2] wore off those things, in a few days, and forestall the dishonor—You will think no caprice of me—

You said "Dark." I know the Butterfly—and the Lizard—and the Orchis—

Are not those *your* Countrymen?

I am happy to be your scholar, and will deserve the kindness, I cannot repay.

If you truly consent, I recite, now—

Will you tell me my fault, frankly as to yourself, for I had rather wince, than die. Men do not call the surgeon, to commend—the Bone, but to set it, Sir, and fracture within, is more critical. And for this, Preceptor, I shall bring you—Obedience—the Blossom from my Garden, and every gratitude I know. Perhaps you smile at me. I could not stop for that—My Business is Circumference—An ignorance, not of Customs, but if caught with the Dawn—or the Sunset see me—Myself the only Kangaroo among the Beauty, Sir, if you please, it afflicts me, and I thought that instruction would take it away.

Because you have much business, beside the growth of me—you will appoint, yourself, how often I shall come—without your inconvenience. And if at any time—you regret you received me, or I prove a different fabric to that you supposed—you must banish me—

When I state myself, as the Representative of the Verse—it does not mean—me—but a supposed person. You are true, about the "perfection."

Today, makes Yesterday mean.

You spoke of Pippa Passes[3]—I never heard anybody speak of Pippa Passes—before.

You see my posture is benighted.

To thank you, baffles me. Are you perfectly powerful? Had I a pleasure you had not, I could delight to bring it.

Your Scholar

---

[1] *Molds* Forms (as with a sculpture); by extension, any pictorial representation of a person.

[2] *the Quick* The living quality. (In the nineteenth century it was common to contrast "the quick" with the dead.)

[3] *Pippa Passes* Dramatic poem (1841) by Robert Browning.

TO OTIS PHILLIPS LORD[4]

[c. 1878]

My lovely Salem[5] smiles at me I seek his Face so often—but I am past disguises (have dropped—) (have done with guises—)

I confess that I love him—I rejoice that I love him—I thank the maker of Heaven and Earth that gave him me to love—the exultation floods me—I can not find my channel—The Creek turned Sea at thoughts of thee—will you punish it—[turn I] involuntary Bankruptcy as the Debtors say. Could that be a Crime—How could that be crime—Incarcerate me in yourself—that will punish me—Threading with you this lovely maze which is not Life or Death tho it has the intangibleness of one and the flush of the other waking for your sake on Day made magical with [before] you before I went to sleep—What pretty phrase—we went to sleep as if it were a country—let us make it one—we could (will) make it one, my native Land—my Darling come oh be a patriot now—Love is a patriot now Gave her life for its (its) country Has it meaning now—Oh nation of the soul thou hast thy freedom now

TO SUSAN GILBERT DICKINSON

[October 1883]

Dear Sue—

The Vision of Immortal Life has been fulfilled—[6]

How simply at the last the Fathom comes! The Passenger and not the Sea, we find surprises us—

Gilbert rejoiced in Secrets—

His Life was panting with them—With what menace of Light he cried "Dont tell, Aunt Emily"! Now my

---

[4] The letter reproduced below is a rough draft; only a fragment of the fair copy remains extant.

[5] *My lovely Salem* Dickinson's nickname for Lord, who resided in Salem, Massachusetts.

[6] *The Vision ... fulfilled—* Dickinson refers in this letter to the recent death of Gilbert, the youngest son of Susan and Austin Dickinson.

ascended Playmate must instruct me. Show us, prattling Preceptor, but the way to thee!

He knew no niggard[1] moment—His Life was full of Boon—The Playthings of the Dervish[2] were not so wild as his—

No Crescent was this Creature—He traveled from the Full—

Such soar, but never set—

I see him in the Star, and meet his sweet velocity in everything that flies—His Life was like the Bugle, which winds itself away, his Elegy an Echo—his Requiem Ecstacy—

Dawn and Meridian[3] in one.

Wherefore would he wait, wronged only of Night, which he left for us—

Without a speculation, our little Ajax[4] spans the whole—

Pass to thy Rendezvous of Light,
Pangless except for us,
Who slowly ford the Mystery
Which thou hast leaped across!

Emily →

Susan Dickinson

Emily Dickinson

---

1 *niggard* Stingy.

2 *Dervish* Sufi Muslim ascetic; dervishes are known for a form of ecstatic religious dancing.

3 *Meridian* I.e., noon.

4 *Ajax* Proverbially strong and courageous hero of Greek mythology, depicted in Homer's *Iliad*.

IN CONTEXT

The Reception of Emily Dickinson in the Nineteenth Century

It has often been assumed that the early reception of Dickinson's poetry was largely unfavorable, or that most reviewers were, at best, uncomfortable with her idiosyncratic style and grammar. In fact, early reviews of *Poems* (1890)—including those by such highly respected critics as Robert Bridges and William Dean Howells—were almost unanimously positive and even laudatory, praising the originality, sensitivity, and force of Dickinson's verse, while often remarking on her reclusiveness and apparent reluctance to publish during her lifetime. Many reviewers took seriously Higginson's claim (in his preface to the volume) that Dickinson's poems were "more suggestive of the poetry of William Blake," the English Romantic poet and visual artist, "than of anything to be elsewhere found." In December 1890, two contributors to the *Critic*, a literary journal based in New York, selected *Poems* as one of "The Best Five Books of the Decade." The volume, indeed, created something of a sensation in the literary world, and by the spring of 1891 was in its sixth printing.

One significant exception to the widespread praise accorded Dickinson was prominent Scottish writer Andrew Lang (1844–1912), who published two highly unfavorable reviews of Dickinson in January 1891; Lang's complaints centered largely on Dickinson's disregard for rhyme as well as on what he called the "nonsense" of her ideas. While Lang was not quite alone in his disapproval, he was very much in the minority.

from Alexander Young, "Boston Letter," *Critic* (11 October 1890)

The volume of "Poems" by the late Emily Dickinson, which Roberts Bros. are to publish next month and which is edited by two of her friends, Mabel Loomis Todd and T.W. Higginson, is of a quality so fine that the wonder is that she had hardly given anything to the world in her lifetime. Having read the advance-sheets I can bear witness to the originality and strength of these poems, their union of profound insight into nature and life with a remarkable vividness of description. They are compact with thought and imagination and have a quaint directness that is emphasized by the neglect of the attractions of form which some of them betray. But the rough diamonds in the collection have a value beyond that of many polished gems of poetry. ...

from anonymous, "From the Book Store," *St. Joseph Daily News* (22 November 1890)

The poems are edited by Mabel Loomis Todd and Col. T.W. Higginson, and are beautifully bound ... in white with silver lilies on the cover, the volume put up in a white embossed box. They are poems of such extraordinary intensity, insight and vividness, and an almost equally startling disregard of poetic laws, that the reader will find himself pursuing almost a new language, and perhaps speculating curiously as to what results would have been insured had the author subjected herself to careful study of poetic ideals—had she learned to chip and polish the marble. It might be that such work as hers would lose in strength rather than gain in melody by such revision.

from anonymous, "New Books," *Boston Post* (27 November 1890)

The editors[1] tell us that the author (who died four years ago at the age of fifty-six) was "a recluse by
… temperament and habit"—a refined and gentle woman, who wrote these verses with absolutely
no thought of publication, but simply to give expression to her deepest feeling. They are, therefore,
introspective with outlooks on Life, Love and Nature, which are most unreal as to their externals but
deeply true in essentials.

Those who like philosophy in verse will easily find it here, but they will probably overlook what is a
finer thing—the original fancy which compresses striking images into a few words, or catches a strange
melody in most irregular measures. One of these delicate fancies is the poem to "The Bee":

> Like trains of cars on tracks of plush
> I hear the level bee;
> A jar across the flower goes,
> Their velvet masonry
> Withstands, until the sweet assault
> Their chivalry consumes,
> While he, victorious, tilts away,
> To vanquish other blooms.

Then, in a vein entirely different from her other verses, is the vivid picture of "some lonely houses, off
the road, a robber'd like the look of—" which is a bit of poetic melodrama that Poe would have liked.

The love poems are written in the attitude of a worshipper and not of a lover—and the exaggeration
is often of a kind that is saved from being absurd by its sincerity. It is not passion, but fervid loyalty that
is depicted—and the chill of intellectual monasticism is in it. There are, however, one or two of the love
poems that are more human and feminine in feeling, of which we may quote what is perhaps the best:

> I'm wife; I've finished that,
> That other state;
> I'm Czar; I'm woman now;
> It's safer so.
> How odd the girl's life looks
> Behind this soft eclipse;
> I think the earth seems so
> To those in heaven now.
> This being comfort then,
> That other kind was pain:
> But why compare?
> I'm wife! stop there!

The volume will delight thoughtful people as the poetic expression of a rare and shy intelligence.

---

[1]   *The editors*   I.e., Todd and Higginson.

from Kinsley Twining and William Hayes Ward, "Poems by Emily Dickinson,"
Independent (11 December 1890)

Whatever may be said as to the merits or demerits of these poems, they bear the stamp of original genius. Making allowance for a certain Emersonian diction,[1] there is nothing like these poems in the language, unless Mr. Higginson's fancy that they resemble William Blake will hold. "H.H."[2] was the poet's chosen and admiring friend, so far as we know the only literary intimate she had; but we detect no traces of "H.H." in these poems. If there are such they wholly fade in the torrent of original passion which could move in no channel but its own. It would be extravagant to say that they are written in a language of their own; but so far as technical execution is concerned, the author invented her poetic idiom. In her eager passion for direct expression, her thought crowds on in fierce impatience of the restraints and limitations of grammar or rhyme. The poetic substance comes to her mind in broad masses, like a painting of the French school,[3] and takes form on her canvas without the minutiae of pen and pencil details. The poems do not take effect on the reader at once; and if they captivate him at all, will do so slowly. Speaking for all but the hopeless conventional ones, we should say they are sure to win him at last. The poems, though numerous, are desultory and brief. They make no attempt at long flight or sustained power. They shoot up high into the sky and drop thence a few notes of uncommon melody, and the song ends, sometimes broken, generally too soon. Mr. Higginson, in his fascinating Preface, calls them flashes; but they are flashes that combine into visions. The portrait he draws of the author and his picture of her life is tender, beautiful and strong as a poem; but it was a life which needed for its interpretation to be seen through these poems. In them the witchery of genius throws its charm and its fascination over what without it would strike the eye as bare singularity. Never did a Puritan maiden weave her bower in such silence and solitude as this lady of Amherst chose for herself. Stranger yet was the passion that swept her breast. …

from William Dean Howells,[4] "Editor's Study," *Harper's New Monthly Magazine*
(January 1891)

… Few of the poems in the book are long, but none of the short, quick impulses of intense feeling or poignant thought can be called fragments. They are each a compassed whole, a sharply finished point, and there is evidence, circumstantial and direct, that the author spared no pains in the perfect expression of her ideals. Nothing, for example, could be added that would say more than she has said in four lines:

> Presentiment is that long shadow on the lawn
> Indicative that suns go down;
> The notice to the startled grass
> That darkness is about to pass.

Occasionally, the outside of the poem, so to speak, is left so rough, so rude, that the art seems to have faltered. But there is apparent to reflection the fact that the artist meant just this harsh exterior to remain,

---

[1]   *Emersonian diction*   Many of the early reviews of Dickinson's poems drew comparisons to the poetry of Emerson—which at the time was both frequently praised for its suggestive power and sometimes disparaged for its lack of clarity.

[2]   *H.H.*   Helen Hunt Jackson (1830–85), a poet and former classmate of Dickinson's.

[3]   *the French school*   Reference to the budding Impressionist movement, which originated in France in the 1870s. Impressionists' paintings were characterized by sketchy brushstrokes and a rejection of conventional subject matter; many of the movement's artists were known for completing paintings very quickly and without preliminary sketches.

[4]   *William Dean Howells*   Prominent American novelist and critic (1837–1920).

and that no grace of smoothness could have imparted her intention as it does. It is the soul of an abrupt, exalted New England woman that speaks in such brokenness. ...

If nothing else had come out of our life but this strange poetry we should feel that in the work of Emily Dickinson America, or New England rather, had made a distinctive addition to the literature of the world, and could not be left out of any record of it; and the interesting and important thing is that this poetry is as characteristic of our life as our business enterprise, our political turmoil, our demagogism, our millionarism. ...

from anonymous, *Springfield Republican* (23 January 1891)

It is true that there has been a remarkable response to this wonderful spiritual verse of Emily
... Dickinson, but it has been accompanied by a vexatious display of the current feebleness of vision among professed critics,[1] who complain of the ragged lines and imperfect rhymes—as if one should complain that every leaf of the rose is not a perfect geometrical figure, or that the rainbow is not definitely bounded by straight chalk marks. ...

from Andrew Lang, "A Literary Causerie," *Speaker* (31 January 1891)

Though few people care for poetry, and though a new poet has to wait long for his laurels[2] in England, in America both singers and the love of song seem much more popular. America has lately lost two great lyrists—lost them before their very names were heard of in our country. One was Miss Emily Dickinson, whose remains Mr. Howells has applauded, and has found to be in themselves a justification of America's literary existence. These poems have reached a third edition: but while the term "edition" now means 100 copies, and now 10,000, this fact tells us very little. Judging Miss Dickinson's work by Mr. Howells' specimens, her muse was *super grammaticum*,[3] and was wholly reckless of rhyme. ...[4]

... Aristotle[5] says that the ultimate Democracy is remarkable for the license it permits to women and to children. Miss Dickinson, like Mrs. Browning,[6] though she was not learned like Mrs. Browning, took great license with rhymes. Possibly the poetry of Democracy will abound more and more in these liberties. But then the question will arise, Is it poetry at all? For poetry, too, has its laws, and if they are absolutely neglected, poetry will die. This may be of no great moment, as there is plenty of old poetry in stock, but still one must urge that lawless poetry is skimble-skamble stuff, with no right to exist. ... What did the corpse mean by "failing for beauty"? Did it die because it was not pretty? Or did it die for love of the beauty of some other person? And, if the dead bodies could go on conversing for a considerable time, why did they relapse into silence when the moss "had reached their lips, and covered up their names"? Moss does not, in fact, grow inside graves, and how could any development of moss on the tombstone affect these conversational corpses? A poem may be nonsense and yet may be charming, like Mr. William Morris's[7] "Blue Closet," which has the inconsequence of a dream. But a poem like the poem of the dead bodies is unrhymed nonsense. ...

---

[1] *professed critics* The *Springfield Republican* (in which several of Dickinson's poems had appeared in the 1860s) appears to have been taking aim at one critic in particular—Andrew Lang, whose long review of Dickinson's *Poems* appeared under the heading "The Newest Poet" in the London *Daily News*, 2 January 1891. (A second piece by Lang on Dickinson, which appeared in the January 1891 issue of the *Speaker*, is excerpted below.)

[2] *laurels* Wreath of bay laurel leaves, a traditional symbol of literary merit.

[3] *super grammaticum* Latin: above grammar.

[4] Lang proceeds to quote from the poem beginning, "I died for beauty."

[5] *Aristotle* Ancient Greek philosopher (384–322 BCE).

[6] *Mrs. Browning* English poet Elizabeth Barrett Browning (1806–61), who was admired by Dickinson.

[7] *Mr. William Morris* English writer and textile designer (1834–96).

The daguerreotype repoduced in the introduction to Dickinson and on page 85 is the only verified photograph of Emily Dickinson known to exist. The original daguerreotype was taken by William C. North between about 1846 and 1848, when the poet was a teenager; it appears that neither Dickinson nor her family were ever satisfied with it as a likeness, and Dickinson was reluctant to share it with outsiders throughout her life. That daguerreotype was retouched by artist Laura Coombs Hills after Dickinson's death upon the request of her sister, Lavinia Dickinson; the resulting image is reproduced here. It was used extensively in the twentieth century, including in Martha Dickinson Bianchi's *The Life and Letters of Emily Dickinson* (1924) and in several mid-century biographies of Dickinson.

THE

ATLANTIC MONTHLY:

A Magazine of Literature, Science, Art, and Politics.

VOL. LXVIII. — OCTOBER, 1891. — No. CCCCVIII.

THE HOUSE OF MARTHA.

XLVIII.

IN A COLD, BARE ROOM.

WHEN I reached Arden, I took one of the melancholy vehicles which stand at our station, and very much astonished the driver by ordering him to take me, not to my own home, but to the House of Martha.

"You know they 're busted up, sir," remarked the man, turning to me, as his old horse hurried us along at his best pace.

"But the sisters have not left?" I eagerly asked.

"Not all," he replied, "but two or three of them went down this morning."

"Drive on quicker," I said. "I am in a hurry."

The man gave the horse a crack with his whip, which made no difference whatever in our speed, and said : "If you 've got a bill agin any of them, sir, you need n't worry. The Mother is still there, and she 's all right, you know."

"Bill! Nonsense !" I answered.

"I 'm sorry they 're busted," said the man. "They did n't do much hackin', but they give us a lot of haulin' from the station."

As I hurried up the broad path which led to the front of the House of Martha, I found the door of the main entrance open, — something I had never seen before, although I had often passed the house. I entered unceremoniously, and saw before me, in the hallway, a woman in gray stooping over a trunk. She turned at the sound of my footsteps on the bare floor, and I beheld Sister Sarah. Her eyes flashed as she saw me, and I know that her first impulse was to order me out of the house ; but this, of course, she now had no right to do, yet there were private rights which she still maintained.

"I should think," she said, "that a man who has done all the mischief you have done — who has worked and planned and plotted and contrived until he has undermined and utterly ruined a sisterhood of pious women who ask nothing of this world but to be let alone to do their own work in their own way, would be ashamed to put his nose into this house ; but I suppose a man who would do what you have done does not know what shame is. Have you come here to sneer and gibe and scorn and mock and gloat over the misfortunes of the women whose home you have broken up, ruined, and devastated ? "

"Madam," I replied, "can you tell me where I can find Miss Sylvia Raynor ? "

She looked as if she were about to spring and bite.

"Atrocious ! " she exclaimed. "I will not stay under the same roof with you." And she marched out of the door.

I made my way into the reception-room. I met no one, and the room was empty, although I heard on the floor above the sound of many footsteps, apparently those of the sisters preparing for departure.

EMILY DICKINSON'S LETTERS.

FEW events in American literary history have been more curious than the sudden rise of Emily Dickinson into a posthumous fame only more accentuated by the utterly recluse character of her life and by her aversion to even a literary publicity. The lines which form a prelude to the published volume of her poems are the only ones that have yet come to light indicating even a temporary desire to come in contact with the great world of readers ; she seems to have had no reference, in all the rest, to anything but her own thought and a few friends. But for her only sister, it is very doubtful if her poems would ever have been printed at all ; and when published, they were launched quietly and without any expectation of a wide audience ; yet the outcome of it is that six editions of the volume have been sold within six months, a suddenness of success almost without a parallel in American literature.

One result of this glare of publicity has been a constant and earnest demand by her readers for further information in regard to her ; and I have decided with much reluctance to give some extracts from her early correspondence with one whom she always persisted in regarding — with very little ground for it — as a literary counselor and confidant.

It seems to be the opinion of those who have examined her accessible correspondence most widely, that no other letters bring us quite so intimately near to the peculiar quality and aroma of her nature ; and it has been urged upon me very strongly that her readers have the right to know something more of this gifted and most interesting woman.

On April 16, 1862, I took from the post office in Worcester, Mass., where I was then living, the following letter : —

MR. HIGGINSON, — Are you too deeply occupied to say if my verse is alive ?

The mind is so near itself it cannot see distinctly, and I have none to ask.

Should you think it breathed, and had you the leisure to tell me, I should feel quick gratitude.

If I make the mistake, that you dared to tell me would give me sincerer honor toward you.

I inclose my name, asking you, if you please, sir, to tell me what is true ?

That you will not betray me it is needless to ask, since honor is its own pawn.

The letter was postmarked "Amherst," and it was in a handwriting so peculiar that it seemed as if the writer might have taken her first lessons by studying the famous fossil bird-tracks in the museum of that college town. Yet it was not in the slightest degree illiterate, but cultivated, quaint, and wholly unique. Of punctuation there was little ; she used chiefly dashes, and it has been thought better, in printing these letters, as with her poems, to give them the benefit in this respect of the ordinary usages ; and so with her habit as to capitalization, as the printers call it, in which she followed the Old English and present German method of thus distinguishing every noun substantive. But the most curious thing about the letter was the total absence of a signature. It proved, however, that she had written her name on a card, and put it under the shelter of a smaller envelope inclosed in the larger ; and even this name was written — as if the shy writer wished to recede as far as possible from view — in pencil, not in ink. The name was Emily Dickinson. Inclosed with the letter were four poems, two of which have been already printed, — "Safe in their alabaster cham-

Pages from the October 1891 issue of *The Atlantic Monthly*.

Thomas Wentworth Higginson

IN CONTEXT

Thomas Wentworth Higginson, "Emily Dickinson's Letters"

Thomas Wentworth Higginson (1823–1911) was a Unitarian minister, women's rights activist, abolitionist, and frequent contributor to *The Atlantic Monthly*, where he wrote essays on various topics, including literature and the arts, nature, and contemporary political events. Emily Dickinson first wrote to him in April 1862 in response to his article "Letter to a Young Contributor," in which he had provided advice to aspiring writers. This initiated a correspondence that would last until Dickinson's death; she would meet Higginson in person only twice. Both writers appear to have had a great deal of respect and regard for one another. In October 1891, five years after Dickinson's death and almost one year after the publication of the first volume of her *Poems*, *The Atlantic Monthly* featured an article by Higginson in which he reflected on their twenty-four-year-long correspondence, quoting extensively from her letters. (None of Higginson's letters to Dickinson have survived.) That article is reproduced below; a small selection of Dickinson's letters to Higginson are also reproduced above, pages 81–83. As in his edition of her *Poems*, Higginson has here edited Dickinson's letters to bring them more closely in line with nineteenth-century style conventions.

Thomas Wentworth Higginson, "Emily Dickinson's Letters," *The Atlantic Monthly* (October 1891)

Few events in American literary history have been more curious than the sudden rise of Emily Dickinson into a posthumous fame only more accentuated by the utterly recluse character of her life and by her aversion to even a literary publicity. The lines which form a prelude to the published volume of her poems[1] are the only ones that have come to light indicating even a temporary desire to come in contact with the great world of readers; she seems to have had no reference, in all the rest, to anything but her own thought and a few friends. But for her only sister[2] it is very doubtful if her poems would ever have been printed at all; and when published, they were launched quietly and without any expectation of a wide audience; yet the outcome of it is that six editions of the volume have been sold within six months, a suddenness of success almost without a parallel in American literature.

One result of this glare of publicity has been a constant and earnest demand by her readers for further information in regard to her; and I have decided with much reluctance to give some extracts from her early correspondence with one whom she always persisted in regarding—with very little ground for it—as a literary counselor and confidant.

It seems to be the opinion of those who have examined her accessible correspondence most widely, that no other letters bring us quite so intimately near to the peculiar quality and aroma of her nature; and it has been urged upon me very strongly that her readers have the right to know something more of this gifted and most interesting woman.

On April 16, 1862, I took from the post office in Worcester, Mass., where I was then living, the following letter:

> MR. HIGGINSON—Are you too deeply occupied to say if my verse is alive?
> The mind is so near itself it cannot see distinctly, and I have none to ask.
> Should you think it breathed, and had you the leisure to tell me, I should feel quick gratitude.

---

[1]   *The lines ... her poems*   In their 1890 collection of Dickinson's *Poems*, Todd and Higginson chose the poem beginning "This is my letter to the world" as the volume's "Prelude."

[2]   *only sister*   Lavinia Norcross Dickinson (1833–99), who discovered Dickinson's fascicles after her death.

If I make the mistake, that you dared to tell me would give me sincerer honor toward you.

I enclose my name, asking you, if you please, sir, to tell me what is true?

That you will not betray me it is needless to ask, since honor is its own pawn.

The letter was postmarked "Amherst," and it was in a handwriting so peculiar that it seemed as if the writer might have taken her first lessons by studying the famous fossil bird-tracks in the museum of that college town. Yet it was not in the slightest degree illiterate, but cultivated, quaint, and wholly unique. Of punctuation there was little; she used chiefly dashes, and it has been thought better, in printing these letters, as with her poems, to give them the benefit in this respect of the ordinary usages; and so with her habit as to capitalization, as the printers call it, in which she followed the Old English and present German method of thus distinguishing every noun substantive. But the most curious thing about the letter was the total absence of a signature. It proved, however, that she had written her name on a card, and put it under the shelter of a smaller envelope enclosed in the larger; and even this name was written—as if the shy writer wished to recede as far as possible from view—in pencil, not in ink. The name was Emily Dickinson. Enclosed with the letter were four poems, two of which have been already printed—"Safe in their alabaster chambers" and "I'll tell you how the sun rose," together with the two that here follow. The first comprises in its eight lines a truth so searching that it seems a condensed summary of the whole experience of a long life:

> We play at paste[1]
> Till qualified for pearl;
> Then drop the paste
> And deem ourself a fool.
>
> The shapes, though, were similar
> And our new hands
> Learned gem-tactics,
> Practicing sands.

Then came one which I have always classed among the most exquisite of her productions, with a singular felicity of phrase and an aerial lift that bears the ear upward with the bee it traces:

> The nearest dream recedes unrealized.
> The heaven we chase,
> Like the June bee
> Before the schoolboy,
> Invites the race,
> Stoops to an easy clover,
> Dips—evades—teases—deploys—
> Then to the royal clouds
> Lifts his light pinnace,[2]
> Heedless of the boy
> Staring, bewildered, at the mocking sky.
>
> Homesick for steadfast honey—
> Ah! the bee flies not
> Which brews that rare variety.

---

[1]   *paste*   Cut glass used to make imitation jewels.

[2]   *pinnace*   Small ship.

The impression of a wholly new and original poetic genius was as distinct on my mind at the first reading of these four poems as it is now, after thirty years of further knowledge; and with it came the problem never yet solved, what place ought to be assigned in literature to what is so remarkable, yet so elusive of criticism. The bee himself did not evade the schoolboy more than she evaded me; and even at this day I still stand somewhat bewildered, like the boy.

Circumstances, however, soon brought me in contact with an uncle of Emily Dickinson, a gentleman not now living; a prominent citizen of Worcester, a man of integrity and character, who shared her abruptness and impulsiveness but certainly not her poetic temperament, from which he was indeed singularly remote. He could tell but little of her, she being evidently an enigma to him, as to me. It is hard to tell what answer was made by me, under these circumstances, to this letter. It is probable that the adviser sought to gain time a little and find out with what strange creature he was dealing. I remember to have ventured on some criticism which she afterwards called "surgery," and on some questions, part of which she evaded, as will be seen, with a naive skill such as the most experienced and worldly coquette might envy. Her second letter (received April 26, 1862) was as follows:

> MR. HIGGINSON—Your kindness claimed earlier gratitude, but I was ill, and write today from my pillow.
>
> Thank you for the surgery;[1] it was not so painful as I supposed. I bring you others, as you ask, though they might not differ. While my thought is undressed, I can make the distinction; but when I put them in the gown, they look alike and numb.
>
> You asked how old I was? I made no verse, but one or two, until this winter, sir.
>
> I had a terror since September,[2] I could tell to none; and so I sing, as the boy does by the burying ground, because I am afraid.
>
> You inquire my books. For poets, I have Keats, and Mr. and Mrs. Browning.[3] For prose, Mr. Ruskin, Sir Thomas Browne, and the Revelations.[4] I went to school, but in your manner of the phrase had no education. When a little girl, I had a friend who taught me Immortality; but venturing too near, himself, he never returned. Soon after my tutor died, and for several years my lexicon was my only companion. Then I found one more, but he was not contented I be his scholar, so he left the land.
>
> You ask of my companions. Hills, sir, and the sundown, and a dog large as myself, that my father bought me. They are better than beings[5] because they know, but do not tell; and the noise in the pool at noon excels my piano.
>
> I have a brother and sister; my mother does not care for thought, and father, too busy with his briefs[6] to notice what we do. He buys me many books, but begs me not to read them, because he fears they joggle the mind. They[7] are religious, except me, and address an eclipse, every morning, whom they call their "Father."

---

1   *surgery* I.e., Higginson's critiques of the poems Dickinson had sent him with her previous letter.

2   *I had ... since September* It is unclear what "terror" Dickinson is referring to here, though biographers have posited a number of physical and psychological afflictions.

3   *Keats* English Romantic poet John Keats (1795–1821); *Mr. and Mrs. Browning* Married English poets Robert and Elizabeth Browning (1812–89 and 1806–61, respectively).

4   *Mr. Ruskin* English art critic and philosopher John Ruskin (1819–1900); *Sir Thomas Browne* English scientist and theologian (1605–82); *the Revelations* Final book of the New Testament; Revelations is an esoteric and prophetic text which describes, among many things, the eventual second coming of Christ.

5   *beings* I.e., human beings.

6   *briefs* Legal documents (Dickinson's father was a lawyer).

7   *They* I.e., Dickinson's parents and siblings.

But I fear my story fatigues you. I would like to learn. Could you tell me how to grow, or is it unconveyed, like melody or witchcraft?

You speak of Mr. Whitman.[1] I never read his book, but was told that it was disgraceful.

I read Miss Prescott's Circumstance,[2] but it followed me in the dark, so I avoided her.

Two editors of journals came to my father's house this winter, and asked me for my mind, and when I asked them "why" they said I was penurious,[3] and they would use it for the world.

I could not weigh myself, myself. My size felt small to me. I read your chapters in the Atlantic, and experienced honor for you. I was sure you would not reject a confiding question.

Is this, sir, what you asked me to tell you? Your friend,

E. DICKINSON

It will be seen that she had now drawn a step nearer, signing her name, and as my "friend." It will also be noticed that I had sounded her about certain American authors, then much read; and that she knew how to put her own criticisms in a very trenchant way. With this letter came some more verses, still in the same birdlike script, as for instance the following:

> Your riches taught me poverty,
>   Myself a millionaire
> In little wealths, as girls could boast,
>   Till, broad as Buenos Ayre,[4]
> You drifted your dominions
>   A different Peru,
> And I esteemed all poverty
>   For life's estate, with you.
>
> Of mines, I little know, myself,
>   But just the names of gems,
> The colors of the commonest,
>   And scarce of diadems
> So much that, did I meet the queen
>   Her glory I should know;
> But this must be a different wealth,
>   To miss it, beggars so.
>
> I'm sure 'tis India, all day,
>   To those who look on you

---

[1] *Mr. Whitman*   Walt Whitman (1819–92), American poet. The first edition of his collection *Leaves of Grass* was published in 1855; it was well received by many but also scandalized a number of more conservative readers, who were troubled by what they saw as its obscenity as well as by its highly unconventional form.

[2] *Circumstance*   Short story by American writer Harriet Elizabeth Prescott Spofford, published in *The Atlantic Monthly* in 1860; the story's unnamed female protagonist is pursued through the dark woods by a figure referred to as the "Indian Devil."

[3] *penurious*   Poor.

[4] *Buenos Ayre*   Buenos Aires, here representing the wealth of South America, whose mines of gems and silver had been much discussed in American periodicals during this period; the other place names of this poem, "Peru" and "India," share this association with riches and splendor and were considered sources of exotic luxuries.

Without a stint, without a blame,
      Might I but be the Jew![1]
I'm sure it is Golconda[2]
      Beyond my power to deem,
To have a smile for mine, each day,
      How better than a gem!

At least, it solaces to know
      That there exists a gold
Although I prove it just in time
      Its distance to behold;
Its far, far treasure to surmise
      And estimate the pearl
That slipped my simple[3] fingers through
      While just a girl at school!

Here was already manifest that defiance of form, never through carelessness, and never precisely from whim, which so marked her. The slightest change in the order of word—thus, "While yet at school, a girl"—would have given her a rhyme for this last line; but no; she was intent upon her thought, and it would not have satisfied her to make the change. The other poem further showed, what had already been visible, a rare and delicate sympathy with the life of nature:

A bird came down the walk;
He did not know I saw;
He bit an angle-worm[4] in halves
And ate the fellow, raw.

And then he drank a dew
From a convenient grass,
And then hopped sidewise to a wall,
To let a beetle pass.

He glanced with rapid eyes
That hurried all around;
They looked like frightened beads, I thought;
He stirred his velvet head

Like one in danger; cautious.
I offered him a crumb,
And he unrolled his feathers
And rowed him softer home

---

[1] *Jew* Stereotypes in Dickinson's day often depicted Jewish people as merchants of precious gems.

[2] *Golconda* Region in India known for its diamond mines.

[3] *simple* Innocent, foolish.

[4] *angle-worm* Earthworm (like those used by "anglers," or fishers).

Than oars divide the ocean,
Too silver[1] for a seam—
Or butterflies, off banks of noon,
Leap, plashless as they swim.

It is possible that in a second letter I gave more of distinct praise or encouragement, for her third is in a different mood. This was received June 8, 1862. There is something startling in its opening image; and in the yet stranger phrase that follows, where she apparently uses "mob" in the sense of chaos or bewilderment:

DEAR FRIEND—Your letter gave no drunkenness, because I tasted rum before. Domingo[2] comes but once; yet I have had few pleasures so deep as your opinion, and if I tried to thank you, my tears would block my tongue.

My dying tutor told me that he would like to live till I had been a poet, but Death was much of mob as I could master, then. And when, far afterward, a sudden light on orchards, or a new fashion in the wind troubled my attention, I felt a palsy,[3] here, the verses just relieve.

Your second letter surprised me, and for a moment, swung. I had not supposed it. Your first gave no dishonor, because the true are not ashamed. I thanked you for your justice, but could not drip the bells whose jingling cooled my tramp. Perhaps the balm seemed better, because you bled me first. I smile when you suggest that I delay "to publish," that being foreign to my thought as firmament to fin.[4]

If fame belonged to me, I could not escape her; if she did not, the longest day would pass me on the chase, and the approbation of my dog would forsake me then. My barefoot rank is better.

You think my gait "spasmodic." I am in danger, sir. You think me "uncontrolled." I have no tribunal.

Would you have time to be the "friend" you should think I need? I have a little shape: it would not crowd your desk, nor make much racket as the mouse that dents your galleries.

If I might bring you what I do—not so frequent to trouble you—and ask you if I told it clear, 'twould be control to me. The sailor cannot see the North, but knows the needle[5] can. The "hand you stretch me in the dark" I put mine in, and turn away. I have no Saxon[6] now:

And if I asked a common alms,[7]
And in my wondering hand

---

[1]   *silver*   Glistening and in motion, like quicksilver (mercury), as well as silver in color. Dickinson describes the ocean in similar terms elsewhere, for example as an "everywhere of silver."

[2]   *Domingo*   Dickinson may be referring either to the capital city of the Dominican Republic or to the country of Haiti (which had formerly been known as "Saint-Domingue"), for which "Domingo" remained common shorthand in the United States during the nineteenth century. "Domingo" often specifically referenced the Haitian Revolution of 1791, which had resulted in the abolition of slavery and in the expulsion of most French colonials from the country. Both Haiti and the Dominican Republic were (and are) prominent producers of rum.

[3]   *palsy*   Tremor or paralysis.

[4]   *firmament*   The sky or heavens;   *fin*   Fish.

[5]   *needle*   I.e., the needle of a compass.

[6]   *Saxon*   I.e., the English language (which is largely derived from Anglo-Saxon); Dickinson may intend here to refer specifically to prose.

[7]   *alms*   Charity.

A stranger pressed a kingdom,
And I, bewildered, stand;
As if I asked the Orient
Had it for me a morn,
And it should lift its purple dikes
And shatter me with dawn!

But, will you be my preceptor,[1] Mr. Higginson?

With this came the poem already published in her volume and entitled Renunciation;[2] and also that beginning "Of all the sounds dispatched abroad," thus fixing approximately the date of those two. I must soon have written to ask her for her picture, that I might form some impression of my enigmatical correspondent. To this came the following reply, in July, 1862:

Could you believe me without? I had no portrait, now, but am small, like the wren; and my hair is bold, like the chestnut bur; and my eyes, like the sherry in the glass, that the guest leaves. Would this do just as well?

It often alarms father. He says death might occur, and he has moulds[3] of all the rest, but has no mould of me; but I noticed the quick[4] wore off those things, in a few days, and forestall the dishonor. You will think no caprice of me.

You said "Dark." I know the butterfly, and the lizard, and the orchis. Are not those your countrymen?

I am happy to be your scholar, and will deserve the kindness I cannot repay.

If you truly consent, I recite now. Will you tell me my fault, frankly as to yourself, for I had rather wince than die. Men do not call the surgeon to commend the bone, but to set it, sir, and fracture within is more critical. And for this, preceptor, I shall bring you obedience, the blossom from my garden, and every gratitude I know.

Perhaps you smile at me. I could not stop for that. My business is circumference. An ignorance, not of customs, but if caught with the dawn, or the sunset see me, myself the only kangaroo among the beauty, sir, if you please, it afflicts me, and I thought that instruction would take it away.

Because you have much business, beside the growth of me, you will appoint, yourself, how often I shall come, without your inconvenience.

And if at any time you regret you received me, or I prove a different fabric to that you supposed, you must banish me.

When I state myself, as the representative of the verse, it does not mean me, but a supposed person.

You are true about the "perfection." Today makes Yesterday mean.

You spoke of Pippa Passes.[5] I never heard anybody speak of Pippa Passes before. You see my posture is benighted.

To thank you baffles me. Are you perfectly powerful? Had I a pleasure you had not, I could delight to bring it.

                                                    YOUR SCHOLAR

---

1 *preceptor* Teacher.

2 *Renunciation* This poem begins with the line, "There came a day at summer's full."

3 *moulds* Forms (as with a sculpture); by extension, any pictorial representation of a person.

4 *the quick* The living quality. (In the nineteenth century it was common to contrast "the quick" with the dead.)

5 *Pippa Passes* Dramatic poem (1841) by Robert Browning.

This was accompanied by this strong poem, with its breathless conclusion. The title is of my own giving:

THE SAINTS' REST

Of tribulation, these are they,
    Denoted by the white;
The spangled gowns, a lesser rank
    Of victors designate.

All these did conquer; but the ones
    Who overcame most times,
Wear nothing commoner than snow,
    No ornaments but palms.[1]

"Surrender" is a sort unknown
    On this superior soil;
"Defeat" an outgrown anguish,
    Remembered as the mile

Our panting ancle barely passed
    When night devoured the road;
But we stood whispering in the house,
    And all we said, was "Saved!"

[Note by the writer of the verses: I spelled ankle wrong.]

It would seem that at first I tried a little—a very little—to lead her in the direction of rules and traditions; but I fear it was only perfunctory, and that she interested me more in her—so to speak—unregenerate condition. Still, she recognizes the endeavor. In this case, as will be seen, I called her attention to the fact that while she took pains to correct the spelling of a word, she was utterly careless of greater irregularities. It will be seen by her answer that with her usual naive adroitness she turns my point:

DEAR FRIEND—Are these more orderly? I thank you for the truth.
    I had no monarch in my life, and cannot rule myself; and when I try to organize, my little force explodes and leaves me bare and charred.
    I think you called me "wayward." Will you help me improve?
    I suppose the pride that stops the breath, in the core of woods, is not of ourself.
    You say I confess the little mistake, and omit the large. Because I can see orthography; but the ignorance out of sight is my preceptor's charge.
    Of "shunning men and women," they talk of hallowed things, aloud, and embarrass my dog. He and I don't object to them, if they'll exist their side. I think Carlo would please you. He is dumb,[2] and brave. I think you would like the chestnut tree I met in my walk. It hit my notice suddenly, and I thought the skies were in blossom.
    Then there's a noiseless noise in the orchard that I let persons hear.

---

[1] *palms* Traditional symbols of victory.

[2] *dumb* Mute; i.e., does not speak.

You told me in one letter you could not come to see me "now," and I made no answer; not because I had none, but did not think myself the price that you should come so far.

I do not ask so large a pleasure, lest you might deny me.

You say, "Beyond your knowledge." You would not jest with me, because I believe you; but, preceptor, you cannot mean it?

All men say "What" to me, but I thought it a fashion.

When much in the woods, as a little girl, I was told that the snake would bite me, that I might pick a poisonous flower, or goblins kidnap me; but I went along and met no one but angels, who were far shyer of me than I could be of them, so I haven't that confidence in fraud which many exercise.

I shall observe your precept, though I don't understand, always.

I marked a line in one verse, because I met it after I made it, and never consciously touch a paint mixed by another person.

I did not let go it, because it is mine. Have you the portrait of Mrs. Browning?[1]

Persons sent me three. If you had none, will you have mine?

YOUR SCHOLAR

A month or two after this I entered the volunteer army of the civil war, and must have written to her during the winter of 1862–3 from South Carolina or Florida, for the following reached me in camp:

AMHERST

DEAR FRIEND—I did not deem that planetary forces annulled, but suffered an exchange of territory, or world.

I should have liked to see you before you became improbable. War feels to me an oblique place. Should there be other summers, would you perhaps come?

I found you were gone, by accident, as I find systems are, or seasons of the year, and obtain no cause, but suppose it a treason of progress that dissolves as it goes. Carlo still remained, and I told him

Best gains must have the losses' test,
To constitute them gains.

My shaggy ally assented.

Perhaps death gave me awe for friends, striking sharp and early, for I held them since in a brittle love, of more alarm than peace. I trust you may pass the limit of war; and though not reared to prayer, when service is had in church for our arms, I include yourself. . . . I was thinking today, as I noticed, that the "Supernatural" was only the Natural disclosed.

Not "Revelation" 't is that waits,
But our unfurnished eyes.

But I fear I detain you. Should you, before this reaches you, experience immortality,[2] who will inform me of the exchange? Could you, with honor, avoid death, I entreat you sir. It would bereave

YOUR GNOME

I trust the "Procession of Flowers" was not a premonition.

---

[1]   *Mrs. Browning*   English poet Elizabeth Barrett Browning (1806–61).

[2]   *experience immortality*   Die.

I cannot explain this extraordinary signature, substituted for the now customary "Your Scholar," unless she imagined her friend to be in some incredible and remote condition, imparting its strangeness to her. Mr. Howells reminds me that Swedenborg[1] somewhere has an image akin to her "oblique place," where he symbolizes evil as simply an oblique angle. With this letter came verses, most refreshing in that clime of jasmines and mocking-birds, on the familiar robin:

THE ROBIN

The robin is the one
That interrupts the morn
With hurried, few, express reports
When March is scarcely on.

The robin is the one
That overflows the noon
With her cherubic quantity,
An April but begun.

The robin is the one
That, speechless from her nest,
Submits that home and certainty
And sanctity are best.

In the summer of 1863 I was wounded, and in hospital for a time, during which came this letter in pencil, written from what was practically a hospital for her, though only for weak eyes:

DEAR FRIEND—Are you in danger? I did not know that you were hurt. Will you tell me more? Mr. Hawthorne died.[2]

I was ill since September, and since April in Boston for a physician's care. He does not let me go, yet I work in my prison, and make guests for myself.

Carlo did not come, because that he would die in jail; and the mountains I could not hold now, so I brought but the Gods.

I wish to see you more than before I failed. Will you tell me your health? I am surprised and anxious since receiving your note.

The only news I know
Is bulletins all day
From Immortality.

Can you render my pencil? The physician has taken away my pen.
I inclose the address from a letter, lest my figures fail.
Knowledge of your recovery would excel my own.

E. DICKINSON

---

[1] *Mr. Howells* William Dean Howells (1837–1920), American novelist; *Swedenborg* Emanuel Swedenborg (1688–1772), Swedish philosopher, mystic, and mathematician.

[2] *Mr. Hawthorne died* American writer Nathaniel Hawthorne, a native of Massachusetts, died on 19 May 1864. (Higginson was presumably still in hospital at this point.)

Later this arrived:

> DEAR FRIEND—I think of you so wholly that I cannot resist to write again, to ask if you are safe? Danger is not at first, for then we are unconscious, but in the after, slower days.
>
> Do not try to be saved, but let redemption find you, as it certainly will. Love is its own rescue; for we, at our supremest, are but its trembling emblems.
>
> YOUR SCHOLAR

These were my earliest letters from Emily Dickinson, in their order. From this time and up to her death (May 15, 1886) we corresponded at varying intervals, she always persistently keeping up this attitude of "Scholar," and assuming on my part a preceptorship which it is almost needless to say did not exist. Always glad to hear her "recite," as she called it, I soon abandoned all attempt to guide in the slightest degree this extraordinary nature, and simply accepted her confidences, giving as much as I could of what might interest her in return.

Sometimes there would be a long pause, on my part, after which would come a plaintive letter, always terse, like this:

Did I displease you? But won't you tell me how?

Or perhaps the announcement of some event, vast to her small sphere, as this:

AMHERST

Carlo died.

E. DICKINSON

Would you instruct me now?

Or sometimes there would arrive an exquisite little detached strain, every word a picture, like this:

THE HUMMING-BIRD

A route of evanescence
With a revolving wheel;
A resonance of emerald;
A rush of cochineal.[1]
And every blossom on her bush
Adjusts its tumbled head—
The mail from Tunis,[2] probably,
An easy morning's ride.

Nothing in literature, I am sure, so condenses into a few words that gorgeous atom of life and fire of which she here attempts the description. It is, however, needless to conceal that many of her brilliant fragments were less satisfying. She almost always grasped whatever she sought, but with some fracture of grammar and dictionary on the way. Often, too, she was obscure and sometimes inscrutable; and though obscurity is sometimes, in Coleridge's[3] phrase, a compliment to the reader, yet it is never safe to press this compliment too hard.

---

[1] *cochineal* Bright scarlet dye derived from an insect, the *coccus cacti*.

[2] *Tunis* Capital city of Tunisia.

[3] *Coleridge* English Romantic poet Samuel Taylor Coleridge (1772–1834); it is unclear which phrase of Coleridge's Higginson is referring to here, though Coleridge does repeatedly discuss poetic "obscurity" (by which he means ambiguity or lack of clarity) in his classic work of literary criticism, *Biographia Literaria* (1817).

Sometimes, on the other hand, her verses found too much favor for her comfort, and she was urged to publish. In such cases I was sometimes put forward as a defense; and the following letter was the fruit of some such occasion:

> DEAR FRIEND—Thank you for the advice. I shall implicitly follow it.
>
> The one who asked me for the lines I had never seen.
>
> He spoke of "a charity." I refused, but did not inquire. He again earnestly urged, on the ground that in that way I might "aid unfortunate children." The name of "child" was a snare to me, and I hesitated, choosing my most rudimentary, and without criterion.
>
> I inquired of you. You can scarcely estimate the opinion to one utterly guideless. Again thank you.
>
> YOUR SCHOLAR

Again came this, on a similar theme:

> DEAR FRIEND—Are you willing to tell me what is right? Mrs. Jackson, of Colorado[1] ["H. H.," her early schoolmate], was with me a few moments this week, and wished me to write for this. [A circular of the "No Name Series"[2] was enclosed.] I told her I was unwilling, and she asked me why? I said I was incapable, and she seemed not to believe me and asked me not to decide for a few days. Meantime, she would write me. She was so sweetly noble, I would regret to estrange her, and if you would be willing to give me a note saying you disapproved it, and thought me unfit, she would believe you. I am sorry to flee so often to my safest friend, but hope he permits me.

In all this time—nearly eight years—we had never met, but she had sent invitations like the following:

> AMHERST
>
> DEAR FRIEND—Whom my dog understood could not elude others.[3]
>
> I should be so glad to see you, but think it an apparitional pleasure, not to be fulfilled. I am uncertain of Boston.
>
> I had promised to visit my physician for a few days in May, but father objects because he is in the habit of me.
>
> Is it more far to Amherst?
>
> You will find a minute host, but a spacious welcome. . . .[4]
>
> If I still entreat you to teach me, are you much displeased? I will be patient, constant, never reject your knife, and should my slowness goad you, you knew before myself that
>
> > Except the smaller size
> > No lives are round.

---

[1] *Mrs. Jackson, of Colorado* Helen Hunt Jackson (1830–85), novelist, poet, and former classmate of Dickinson's; Jackson had hoped to be named Dickinson's literary executor, but Jackson died first. She resided in Colorado and California later in her life.

[2] *No Name Series* Literary magazine (or "circular") published between 1876 and 1887, whose entries were published anonymously; Helen Hunt Jackson became a regular contributor to the series.

[3] *Whom my dog . . . others* This letter was sent to Higginson shortly after Dickinson's announcement that Carlo had died, in early 1866.

[4] . . . The ellipsis here is Higginson's own.

These hurry to a sphere
And show and end.
The larger slower grow
And later hang;
The summers of Hesperides[1]
Are long.

Afterwards, came this:

AMHERST

DEAR FRIEND—

A letter always feels to me like immortality because it is the mind alone without corporeal friend. Indebted in our talk to attitude and accent, there seems a spectral power in thought that walks alone. I would like to thank you for your great kindness, but never try to lift the words which I cannot hold.

Should you come to Amherst, I might then succeed, though gratitude is the timid wealth of those who have nothing. I am sure that you speak the truth, because the noble do, but your letters always surprise me.

My life has been too simple and stern to embarrass any. "Seen of Angels,"[2] scarcely my responsibility.

It is difficult not to be fictitious in so fair a place, but tests' severe repairs are permitted all.

When a little girl I remember hearing that remarkable passage and preferring the "Power," not knowing at the time that "Kingdom" and "Glory" were included.

You noticed my dwelling alone. To an emigrant, country is idle except it be his own. You speak kindly of seeing me; could it please your convenience to come so far as Amherst, I should be very glad, but I do not cross my father's ground to any house or town.

Of our greatest acts we are ignorant. You were not aware that you saved my life. To thank you in person has been since then one of my few requests. . . . You will excuse each that I say, because no one taught me.

At last, after many postponements, on August 16, 1870, I found myself face to face with my hitherto unseen correspondent. It was at her father's house, one of those large, square, brick mansions so familiar in our older New England towns, surrounded by trees and blossoming shrubs without, and within exquisitely neat, cool, spacious, and fragrant with flowers. After a little delay, I heard an extremely faint and pattering footstep like that of a child, in the hall, and in glided, almost noiselessly, a plain, shy little person, the face without a single good feature, but with eyes, as she herself said, "like the sherry the guest leaves in the glass," and with smooth bands of reddish chestnut hair. She had a quaint and nun-like look, as if she might be a German canoness of some religious order, whose prescribed garb was white pique,[3] with a blue net worsted shawl. She came toward me with two day-lilies, which she put in a childlike way into my hand, saying softly, under her breath, "These are my introduction," and adding, also, under her breath, in childlike fashion, "Forgive me if I am frightened; I never see strangers, and hardly know what I say." But soon she began to talk, and thenceforward continued almost constantly; pausing sometimes to

---

[1] *Hesperides*   In Greek mythology, nymphs associated with the sunset.

[2] *Seen of Angels*   See 1 Timothy 3.16: "And without controversy great is the mystery of godliness: God was manifest in the flesh, justified in the Spirit, seen of angels, preached unto the Gentiles, believed on in the world, received up into glory."

[3] *pique*   Stiff, ribbed cotton.

beg that I would talk instead, but readily recommencing when I evaded. There was not a trace of affecta-
tion in all this; she seemed to speak absolutely for her own relief, and wholly without watching its effect
on her hearer. Led on by me, she told much about her early life, in which her father was always the chief
figure—evidently a man of the old type, *la vieille roche*[1] of Puritanism—a man who, as she said, read on
Sunday "lonely and rigorous books"; and who had from childhood inspired her with such awe, that she
never learned to tell time by the clock till she was fifteen, simply because he had tried to explain it to
her when she was a little child, and she had been afraid to tell him that she did not understand, and also
afraid to ask anyone else lest he should hear of it. Yet she had never heard him speak a harsh word, and
it needed only a glance at his photograph to see how truly the Puritan tradition was preserved in him.
He did not wish his children, when little, to read anything but the Bible; and when, one day, her brother
brought her home Longfellow's *Kavanagh*,[2] he put it secretly under the pianoforte cover, made signs to
her, and they both afterwards read it. It may have been before this, however, that a student of her father's
was amazed to find that she and her brother had never heard of Lydia Maria Child,[3] then much read, and
he brought *Letters from New York*, and hid it in the great bush of old-fashioned tree-box beside the front
door. After the first book she thought in ecstasy, "This, then, is a book, and there are more of them." But
she did not find so many as she expected, for she afterwards said to me, "When I lost the use of my eyes,
it was a comfort to think that there were so few real books that I could easily find one to read me all of
them." Afterwards, when she regained her eyes, she read Shakespeare, and thought to herself, "Why is
any other book needed?"

She went on talking constantly and saying, in the midst of narrative, things quaint and aphoristic. "Is
it oblivion or absorption when things pass from our minds?" "Truth is such a rare thing, it is delight-
ful to tell it." "I find ecstasy in living; the mere sense of living is joy enough." When I asked her if she
never felt any want of employment, not going off the grounds and rarely seeing a visitor, she answered,
"I never thought of conceiving that I could ever have the slightest approach to such a want in all future
time"; and then added, after a pause, "I feel that I have not expressed myself strongly enough," although
it seemed to me that she had. She told me of her household occupations, that she made all their bread,
because her father liked only hers; then saying shyly, "And people must have puddings," this very timidly
and suggestively, as if they were meteors or comets. Interspersed with these confidences came phrases so
emphasized as to seem the very wantonness of over-statement, as if she pleased herself with putting into
words what the most extravagant might possibly think without saying, as thus: "How do most people live
without any thought? There are many people in the world—you must have noticed them in the street—
how do they live? How do they get strength to put on their clothes in the morning?" Or this crowning
extravaganza: "If I read a book and it makes my whole body so cold no fire can ever warm me, I know
that is poetry. If I feel physically as if the top of my head were taken off, I know that is poetry. These are
the only ways I know it. Is there any other way?"

I have tried to describe her just as she was, with the aid of notes taken at the time; but this interview
left our relation very much what it was before—on my side an interest that was strong and even affection-
ate, but not based on any thorough comprehension; and on her side a hope, always rather baffled, that I
should afford some aid in solving her abstruse problem of life.

The impression undoubtedly made on me was that of an excess of tension, and of an abnormal life.
Perhaps in time I could have got beyond that somewhat overstrained relation which not my will, but
her needs, had forced upon us. Certainly I should have been most glad to bring it down to the level of
simple truth and everyday comradeship; but it was not altogether easy. She was much too enigmatical a
being for me to solve in an hour's interview, and an instinct told me that the slightest attempt at direct
cross-examination would make her withdraw into her shell; I could only sit still and watch, as one does

---

[1]   *la vieille roche*   French: the old rock.

[2]   *Longfellow's Kavanagh*   1849 novel by prominent American poet Henry Wadsworth Longfellow.

[3]   *Lydia Maria Child*   American novelist, journalist, and abolitionist (1802–80), whose popular *Letters from New York* were written for the *National Anti-Slavery Standard* in the early 1840s; they featured her reflections on matters such as women's rights, current events, and contemporary arts and culture.

in the woods; I must name my bird without a gun, as recommended by Emerson.[1] Under this necessity I had not opportunity to see that human and humorous side of her which is strongly emphasized by her nearer friends, and which shows itself in her quaint and unique description of a rural burglary, contained in the volume of her poems.[2] Hence, even her letters to me show her mainly on her exaltée side; and should a volume of her correspondence ever be printed, it is very desirable that it should contain some of her letters to friends of closer and more familiar intimacy.

After my visit came this letter:

> Enough is so vast a sweetness, I suppose it never occurs, only pathetic counterfeits.
>
> Fabulous to me as the men of the Revelations who "shall not hunger any more."[3] Even the possible has its insoluble particle.
>
> After you went, I took Macbeth and turned to "Birnam Wood." Came twice "To Dunsinane."[4] I thought and went about my work. . . .
>
> The vein cannot thank the artery, but her solemn indebtedness to him, even the stolidest admit, and so of me who try, whose effort leaves no sound.
>
> You ask great questions accidentally. To answer them would be events. I trust that you are safe.
>
> I ask you to forgive me for all the ignorance I had. I find no nomination sweet as your low opinion.
>
> Speak, if but to blame your obedient child.
>
> You told me of Mrs. Lowell's[5] poems. Would you tell me where I could find them, or are they not for sight? An article of yours, too, perhaps the only one you wrote that I never knew. It was about a "Latch." Are you willing to tell me? [Perhaps "A Sketch."]
>
> If I ask too much, you could please refuse. Shortness to live has made me bold. Abroad is close tonight and I have but to lift my hands to touch the "Heights of Abraham."[6]
>
> DICKINSON

When I said, at parting, that I would come again sometime, she replied, "Say, in a long time; that will be nearer. Some time is no time." We met only once again, and I have no express record of the visit. We corresponded for years, at long intervals, her side of the intercourse being, I fear, better sustained; and she sometimes wrote also to my wife, inclosing flowers or fragrant leaves with a verse or two. Once she sent her one of George Eliot's books, I think Middlemarch,[7] and wrote, "I am bringing you a little granite book for you to lean upon." At other times she would send a single poem, such as these:

---

[1]   *Emerson*   American poet and philosopher Ralph Waldo Emerson (1803–82); Higginson alludes to the first line of his poem "Forbearance."

[2]   *her quaint ... her poems*   Higginson may be referring to the poem that begins "I know some lonely houses off the road," included in *Poems* (1890) under the title "The Lonely House."

[3]   *shall not ... any more*   See Revelation 7.16: "They shall hunger no more, neither thirst any more; neither shall the sun light on them, nor any heat."

[4]   *Macbeth ... Dunsinane*   See Shakespeare's *Macbeth* 4.1.105–07, in which the Third Apparition foretells that "Macbeth shall never vanquished be until / Great Birnam Wood to high Dunsinane Hill / Shall come against him." Birnam Wood is a forest in Scotland.

[5]   *Mrs. Lowell*   Probably Maria White Lowell (1821–53), whose poetry was published posthumously by her husband, prominent poet James Russell Lowell (1819–91).

[6]   *Heights of Abraham*   Tourist destination in Derbyshire, England, which includes tours of mines and caves.

[7]   *Middlemarch*   Influential 1871–72 novel by English novelist George Eliot. The lengthy novel was initially published in several volumes; the first one-volume edition appeared in 1874.

THE BLUE JAY

No brigadier throughout the year
So civic as the jay.
A neighbor and a warrior too,
With shrill felicity
Pursuing winds that censure us
A February Day,
The brother of the universe
Was never blown away.
The snow and he are intimate;
I've often seen them play
When heaven looked upon us all
With such severity
I felt apology were due
To an insulted sky
Whose pompous frown was nutriment
To their temerity.
The pillow of this daring head
Is pungent evergreens;
His larder—terse and militant—
Unknown, refreshing things;
His character—a tonic;
His future—a dispute;
Unfair an immortality
That leaves this neighbor out.

THE WHITE HEAT

Dare you see a soul at the white heat?
　　Then crouch within the door;
Red is the fire's common tint,
　　But when the vivid ore

Has sated flame's conditions,
　　Its quivering substance plays
Without a color, but the light
　　Of unanointed blaze.

Least village boasts its blacksmith,
　　Whose anvil's even din
Stands symbol for the finer forge
　　That soundless tugs within,

Refining these impatient ores
　　With hammer and with blaze,
Until the designated light
　　Repudiated the forge.

Then came the death of her father, that strong Puritan father who had communicated to her so much of the vigor of his own nature, and who bought her many books, but begged her not to read them. Mr. Edward Dickinson, after service in the national House of Representatives and other public positions, had become a member of the lower house of the Massachusetts legislature. The session was unusually prolonged, and he was making a speech upon some railway question at noon, one very hot day (July 16, 1874), when he became suddenly faint and sat down. The house adjourned, and a friend walked with him to his lodgings at the Tremont House; where he began to pack his bag for home, after sending for a physician, but died within three hours. Soon afterwards, I received the following letter:

> That last afternoon that my father lived, though with no premonition, I preferred to be with him, and invented an absence for mother, Vinnie [her sister] being asleep. He seemed peculiarly pleased, as I oftenest stayed with myself; and remarked, as the afternoon withdrew, he "would like it not to end."
> His pleasure almost embarrassed me, and my brother coming, I suggested they walk. Next morning I woke him for the train, and saw him no more.
> His heart was pure and terrible, and I think no other like it exists.
> I am glad there is immortality, but would have tested it myself, before entrusting him. Mr. Bowles was with us. With that exception, I saw none. I have wished for you, since my father died, and had you an hour unengrossed, it would be almost priceless. Thank you for your kindness ⁚ . .

Later she wrote:

> When I think of my father's lonely life and lonelier death, there is this redress—
>
> > Take all away;
> > The only thing worth larceny
> > Is left—the immortality.
>
> My earliest friend wrote me the week before he died, "If I live, I will go to Amherst; if I die, I certainly will."
> Is your house deeper off?
>
> YOUR SCHOLAR

A year afterward came this:

> DEAR FRIEND—Mother was paralyzed Tuesday, a year from the evening father died. I thought perhaps you would care.
>
> YOUR SCHOLAR

With this came the following verse, having a curious seventeenth-century flavor:

> A death-blow is a life-blow to some,
> Who, till they died, did not alive become;
> Who, had they lived, had died, but when
> They died, vitality begun.

And later came this kindred memorial of one of the oldest and most faithful friends of the family, Mr. Samuel Bowles of the *Springfield Republican*:

DEAR FRIEND—I felt it shelter to speak to you.

My brother and sister are with Mr. Bowles, who is buried this afternoon.

The last song that I heard—that was, since the birds—was "He leadeth me, he leadeth me; yea though I walk"[1]—then the voices stooped, the arch was so low.

After this added bereavement the inward life of the diminished household became only more concentrated, and the world was held farther and farther away. Yet to this period belongs the following letter, written about 1880, which has more of what is commonly called the objective or external quality than any she ever wrote me; and shows how close might have been her observation and her sympathy, had her rare qualities taken a somewhat different channel:

DEAR FRIEND—I was touchingly reminded of [a child who had died] this morning by an Indian woman with gay baskets and a dazzling baby, at the kitchen door. Her little boy "once died" she said, death to her dispelling him. I asked her what the baby liked, and she said "to step." The prairie before the door was gay with flowers of hay, and I led her in. She argued with the birds, she leaned on clover walls and they fell, and dropped her. With jargon sweeter than a bell, she grappled buttercups, and they sank together, the buttercups the heaviest. What sweetest use of days! 'T was noting some such scene made Vaughan humbly say, "My days that are at best but dim and hoary." I think it was Vaughan....

And these few fragmentary memorials—closing, like every human biography, with funerals, yet with such as were to Emily Dickinson only the stately introduction to a higher life—may well end with her description of the death of the summer she so loved.

As imperceptibly as grief
The summer lapsed away,
Too imperceptibly to last
To feel like perfidy.

A quietness distilled,
As twilight long begun,
Or Nature spending with herself
Sequestered afternoon.

The dusk drew earlier in,
The morning foreign shone,
A courteous yet harrowing grace
As guests that would be gone.

And thus without a wing
Or service of a keel
Our summer made her light escape
Into the Beautiful.

---

[1]   *He leadeth ... I walk*   See Psalm 23.2–4: "He maketh me to lie down in green pastures: he leadeth me beside the still waters. He restoreth my soul: he leadeth me in the paths of righteousness for his name's sake. Yea, though I walk through the valley of the shadow of death, I will fear no evil: for thou art with me; thy rod and thy staff they comfort me."

ACKNOWLEDGMENTS

Images from Amherst Manuscript (Fascicle #80, Set #88, #372) courtesy of Amherst College Archives and Special Collections. Images from *Herbarium*, ca. 1839–46, call no. MS Am 1118.11 (Seq. 26, 32, 35), and Manuscript poems, call no. MS Am 1118.3 (11a, 11b, 11c, 35a, 35b, 38b, 74d, 165a), Houghton Library, Harvard University. Copyright © President and Fellows of Harvard College. Used with permission.

❧

The Broadview Anthology of American Literature is a collaborative undertaking, with significant contributions from the General Editors, from a wide range of other academics, and from Broadview's in-house editorial staff. The Dickinson material was prepared with input from the General Editors and, at Broadview, from Helena Snopek, Nora Ruddock, and Don LePan. Stephanie M. Farrar of the University of Wisconsin reviewed the material and provided helpful comments and suggestions; her assistance is gratefully acknowledged. (Full responsibility for any errors or omissions, however, rests with the publisher.)

INDEX

From the Publisher

A name never says it all, but the word "Broadview" expresses a good deal of the philosophy behind our company. We are open to a broad range of academic approaches and political viewpoints. We pay attention to the broad impact book publishing and book printing has in the wider world; for some years now we have used 100% recycled paper for most titles. Our publishing program is internationally oriented and broad-ranging. Our individual titles often appeal to a broad readership too; many are of interest as much to general readers as to academics and students.

Founded in 1985, Broadview remains a fully independent company owned by its shareholders—not an imprint or subsidiary of a larger multinational.

To order our books or obtain up-to date information, please visit www.broadviewpress.com.

broadview press

www.broadviewpress.com